William N. Bender

Project-Based LEARNING

Differentiating Instruction for the 21st Century

CORWIN
A SAGE Company

371 .36 BENDER   2012

Bender, William N.

Project-based learning

CORWIN
A SAGE Company

FOR INFORMATION:

Corwin

A SAGE Company

2455 Teller Road

Thousand Oaks, California 91320

(800) 233-9936

Fax: (800) 417-2466

www.corwin.com

SAGE Ltd.

1 Oliver's Yard

55 City Road

London, EC1Y 1SP

United Kingdom

SAGE India Pvt. Ltd.

B 1/I 1 Mohan Cooperative Industrial Area

Mathura Road, New Delhi 110 044

India

SAGE Asia-Pacific Pte. Ltd.

3 Church Street

#10-04 Samsung Hub

Singapore 049483

Acquisitions Editor: Jessica Allan

Associate Editor: Allison Scott

Editorial Assistant: Lisa Whitney

Production Editor: Amy Schroller

Copy Editor: Mark Bast

Typesetter: Hurix Systems Pvt Ltd.

Proofreader: Theresa Kay

Indexer: Judy Hunt

Cover Designer: Candice Harman

Permissions Editor: Karen Ehrmann

Cover images:
iStockphoto.Thinkstock
© Johannes Kroemer/Corbis
Digital Vision

Printed in the United States of America

Library of Congress Cataloging-in-Publication Data

Bender, William N.
  Project-based learning : differentiating instruction for the 21st century / William N. Bender.
       p. cm.
  Includes bibliographical references and index.
  ISBN 978-1-4129-9790-4 (pbk.)
  1. Project method in teaching. 2. Individualized instruction. I. Title.

  LB1139.35.P8B46 2012
  371.3'6—dc23

                                    2011050676

This book is printed on acid-free paper.

Certified Chain of Custody
Promoting Sustainable Forestry
www.sfiprogram.org
SFI-01268

SUSTAINABLE FORESTRY INITIATIVE

SFI label applies to text stock

12 13 14 15 16 10 9 8 7 6 5 4 3 2 1

Contents

Acknowledgments

Corwin gratefully acknowledges the contributions of the following reviewers:

Tania E. Dymkowski
District Instructional Support
Hays Consolidated Independent School District
Kyle, TX

Ann Richardson
Coordinator of English and Gifted/AP Programs
Fayette County Schools
Lafayette Educational Center
Fayetteville, GA

Denise Rives
Educational Consultant
Education Service Center Region 18
Midland, TX

Susan Stewart
Assistant Professor
Ashland University
Ashland, OH

Catherine Alaimo Stickney
Director of Curriculum, Instruction, and Assessment
Ashland Public Schools
Ashland, MA

Diane Woodford
Fifth-Grade Teacher
South Sioux City Community Schools
South Sioux City, NE

About the Author

William N. Bender is an international leader who focuses on practical instructional tactics with an emphasis on response to intervention (RTI) and differentiated instruction in general education classes across the grade levels. In particular, Dr. Bender has written more books on RTI than any other author in the world, two of which are best sellers. He has now completed seven books on various aspects of response to intervention, as well as a professional development videotape on that topic. He completes between forty and fifty workshops yearly in the United States, Canada, and the Caribbean. In the fall of 2010, he was selected to work with the Ministry of Education in Bermuda to establish their nationwide RTI framework. One of his recent books, *Beyond the RTI Pyramid*, was a 2010 finalist for the Distinguished Achievement Award for Excellence in Educational Publishing.

Dr. Bender uses practical strategies and easy humor to make his workshops an enjoyable experience for all, and he is frequently asked to return to the same school or district for additional workshops. He consistently receives positive reviews of his professional-development workshops for educators across the grade levels. Dr. Bender believes his job is to inform educators of innovative, up-to-date tactics for the classroom, rooted in current research, in an enjoyable workshop experience. He is able to convey this information in a humorous, motivating fashion.

Dr. Bender began his education career teaching in a junior high school resource classroom, working with adolescents with behavioral disorders and learning disabilities. He earned his Ph.D. in special education from the University of North Carolina and has taught in leading universities around the nation, including Rutgers University and the University of Georgia. He is now consulting and writing full-time and has published more than sixty research articles and twenty-three books in education.

Follow William Bender on Twitter.
Twitter.com/williambender1

Introduction

Project-based learning (PBL) is an instructional model based on having students confront real-world issues and problems that they find meaningful, determine how to address them, and then act in a collaborative fashion to create problem solutions (Barell, 2010; Baron, 2011; Belland, French, & Ertmer, 2009; Larmer & Mergendoller, 2010). As schools in the United States, Canada, and around the world struggle with the implications of developing more effective instructional models in a period of shrinking budgets, many educational advocates have recommended PBL as an effective instructional approach that results in high levels of student engagement and achievement (Barell, 2007; David, 2008; Ghosh, 2010; Laboy-Rush, 2011; Mergendollar, Maxwell, & Bellisimo, 2007).

Project-based learning has become a topic of interest as the emphasis on effective education has increased in recent years. In fact, many educators foresee rather drastic disruptions in the teaching/learning process, brought about by ever-changing technologies, the increasing demands of struggling students, and various changes now underway in education such as increased emphasis on differentiated instruction and the response-to-intervention initiative (Barell, 2010; Bender & Waller, 2011; Bonk, 2010; Laboy-Rush, 2011; Partnership for 21st Century Skills, 2009). In that context, the PBL instructional approach seems very well situated to become the primary model of instruction in the next century, and educators are well advised to get on board with this innovative approach to teaching.

> Project-based learning is an instructional model based on having students confront real-world issues and problems that they find meaningful, determine how to address them, and then act in a collaborative fashion to create problem solutions.

> The PBL instructional approach seems very well situated to become the primary model of instruction in the next century, and educators are well advised to get on board with this innovative approach to teaching.

While project-based learning is not new (Bransford, Sherwood, Vye, & Rieser, 1986), it has recently received increased emphasis as educators and business leaders look for ways to move educator forward and develop students' skills in 21st-century technologies, problem solving, and collaboration (Partnership for 21st Century Skills, 2007, 2009). PBL originated in the early decades of the 1900s (Dewey, 1933) and was originally applied in medical education rather than in public schools (Cote, 2007). However, current applications of PBL look decidedly different from those early applications of the concept, since modern instructional technologies have matured and today play such a definitive role in PBL instruction (Bender & Waller, 2011; Cote, 2007).

About This Book

Today, project-based learning (PBL) is one avenue for differentiated instruction that is strongly recommended for 21st-century classrooms (Barell, 2010; Bender & Waller, 2011; Ghosh, 2010; Laboy-Rush, 2011; Partnership for 21st Century Skills, 2009). Teachers are increasingly applying PBL instruction across the grade levels and are exploring how this instructional approach works in real classrooms. This book will address that question and present practical guidelines on how to use PBL across the curriculum.

However, this book goes much further than earlier efforts. This is one of the first books to explore PBL as an approach to differentiated instruction, one that bases that discussion in modern applications of technology in the classroom. Because many of the earlier books on PBL did not take into account either the concept of differentiated instruction or the ever-evolving technologies that are available for instructional application today, this book is really unique in that approach. Of course most classrooms do not offer all of the modern technologies that can be used in education, so practical implementation guidelines are provided throughout the book for classes with somewhat limited technology resources.

> This is one of the first books to explore PBL as an approach to differentiated instruction, one that bases that discussion in modern applications of technology in the classroom.

Thus, this book interfaces several critical instructional techniques for 21st-century classes—PBL, differentiated instruction, and literacy in 21st-century technology skills. Not only will this book be one of the first modern books on PBL, it will also be the first book to thoroughly explore that cross-fertilization of instructional practices and concepts. While some research is presented and discussed, the primary emphasis of this book will be on modern, practical instructional strategies for elementary grades and in middle and secondary subject areas.

Who Should Read This Book

The book is intended to be a professional development resource book for many in education including the following:

- Practicing teachers,
- Administrators,
- School district personnel,
- Educational leaders,
- College faculty, and
- School board members.

Specifically, the book is intended to assist an individual teacher's move into PBL instruction within his or her class, and while the focus of this book is on an individual teacher's effort, PBL is often undertaken as a schoolwide instructional effort (Barell, 2007). For that reason, the professional learning community or educational leadership team within a school should also feel free to undertake this professional development effort jointly.

Contents and Organization of the Book

Each chapter in this book provides a great deal of information on how PBL works in real classrooms, and multiple examples of actual projects from real schools are provided. Also, much information is highlighted in the boxed sections of the chapters such as guidelines for certain tasks within PBL, steps in the PBL instructional process, research evidence on PBL, assessment options within PBL, and other critical information. Specific strategies are described at length, as are the undergirding theoretical issues, but the major emphasis is on how PBL actually works. Thus, implementation suggestions comprise the key components of this text.

Chapter 1 describes PBL as best-practices instruction, since PBL engages students in their learning tasks so completely. The chapter presents an overview of PBL and various model projects ranging from kindergarten up through high school. An initial discussion of what project-based learning is will be followed by a discussion of several sample PBL projects. Two example projects, a middle school example and an elementary school example, are discussed at length, and one of these involves a webquest and a rubric that is frequently used in evaluation of PBL projects. The chapter also presents many brief descriptions of PBL projects across the grade levels.

Chapter 2 presents a discussion of PBL in the context of the classroom. Teachers must initially consider how PBL fits within their instruction, as either an adjunct to unit-based instruction or as a replacement for unit-based instructional planning. Next, a short section summarizing research on PBL is presented, including research that shows not only the efficacy of this technique relative to traditional instructional models but also the efficacy of PBL for improving students' academic performance on standards-based assessments. Finally, sections on technology within PBL and challenges teachers face as they move into PBL are included.

Chapter 3 presents specific implementation steps for planning and instruction using a PBL model. PBL projects include various elements or components that make up the project assignment, and while various PBL proponents differ on what these are, most agree on the basic overall structure of PBL. This chapter presents those critical PBL components and then describes a step-by-step PBL planning procedure. Another example of a model PBL project is presented as the basis for this discussion.

Chapter 4 focuses on instructional technologies and strategies that facilitate PBL in the classroom, and it describes the most up-to-date teaching tools, such as alternative reality gaming or Ning in the context of PBL. Whereas many teachers are using class blogs, and online webquests today, applications of social networking technologies and emerging mobility technologies are more recent, and these will be discussed in terms of how they might apply for PBL instruction. PBL has long emphasized gaming and simulations as one option for PBL instruction, and those will be described here. Finally, another model PBL project on Civil War studies in middle and high school is presented, with an emphasis on technology applications within PBL instruction.

Chapter 5 describes various nontechnological instructional strategies that fit extremely well within the PBL framework. For example, instruction in strategies that students can repeatedly use in PBL units, strategies such as brainstorming, timeline planning strategies, or metacognitive support strategies are critical in PBL, as are minilessons on specific content that students will find essential in completing the PBL unit. Teaching strategies such as cooperative learning and scaffolded instruction are described in the context of PBL instruction, since PBL is founded on collaborative problem solving. Thus, teachers should maximize the use of these strategies in order to emphasize cooperative tasks within the overall PBL-based curriculum.

Chapter 6 discusses assessment options within PBL. One of the issues teachers face in moving into PBL involves a perceived mismatch between standards-based, direct instruction and project-based learning, though research has demonstrated that students in PBL instructional approaches do better at statewide standardized assessments than their counterparts in more traditional instruction (Geier et al., 2008; Gijbels, Dochy, Van den Bossche, & Segers, 2005; Mergendollar, Maxwell, & Bellisimo, 2007). Still, assessment of student progress is critical in today's classes, and this chapter focuses on the use and application of several assessment tools for PBL, including rubric-based assessment, self-evaluation, peer evaluation, group grading, and portfolio assessment. While there is no specific assessment practice that must be incorporated into PBL, most of the research and practitioner guidelines stress these rather innovative assessment options, either individually or in conjunction with more traditional assessment options, and the advantages and concerns for each approach will be highlighted. A model PBL project is described as the basis for discussion of assessment practices within PBL instruction.

Finally, while the relationship between PBL instruction and the Common Core State Standards (www.corestandards.org/the -standards) is described throughout the text, the appendix presents a discussion of how educational standards in other states likewise correlate with PBL instruction. The appendix uses educational standards from the Texas Educational Agency, specifically, the Texas Essential Knowledge and Skills Standards (TEKS) as an example of a state that did not adopt the Common Core Standards (see http://ritter.tea .state.tx.us/rules/tac/chapter113/ch113b.html#113.18).

Conclusion

As schools struggle to teach all students in a world of limited motivation, poor problem-solving skills, extremely limited budgets, and ever-changing instructional technologies, PBL has emerged as an option for 21st-century classrooms (Baron, 2011; Belland, French, & Ertmer, 2009; Larmer & Mergendoller, 2010; Partnership for 21st Century Skills, 2009). The proponents of PBL are marshalling their resources in an effort to reform schools along these lines, and the evidence does indicate that students respond quite well to this form of instruction.

Further, PBL is now seen by many as the best approach for emphasizing problem-solving skills in a world in which knowledge itself is outdated by the time it is printed in a textbook (Barell, 2010; Belland, French, & Ertmer, 2009; Larmer & Mergendoller, 2010; Partnership for 21st Century Skills, 2009). Thus, teachers are wise to embrace this instructional approach and explore the possibilities it brings for the students in their classrooms. We owe our students the very best education we can provide, and much research indicates that PBL represents best instructional practice today. This is, in every sense, teaching for the 21st century!

1

Engaging Students Through Project-Based Learning

What Is Project-Based Learning?

Project-based learning (PBL) is one of the most effective ways available to engage students with their learning content, and for that reason, PBL is now recommended by many educational leaders as a best instructional practice (Barell, 2010; Baron, 2011; Cole & Wasburn-Moses, 2010; Larmer & Mergendoller, 2010). PBL is an exciting, innovative instructional format in which students select many aspects of their assignment and are motivated by real-world problems that can, and in many cases will, contribute to their community.

PBL may be defined as using authentic, real-world projects, based on a highly motivating and engaging question, task, or problem, to teach students academic content in the context of working cooperatively to solve the problem (Barell, 2007, 2010; Baron, 2011; Grant, 2010). Student inquiry is heavily integrated into project-based learning, and because students typically have some choice in selecting their group's project, and the methods they would use to solve that project, they tend to be more highly motivated to work diligently toward a solution to the problem (Drake & Long, 2009; Maloney, 2010). This typically results in high levels of engagement with the academic content involved in solving the problem or completing the project, as well as higher levels of academic achievement (Grant, 2010; Larner & Mergendoller, 2010; Marzano, 2007).

> PBL may be defined as using authentic, real-world projects, based on a highly motivating and engaging question, task, or problem, to teach students academic content in the context of working cooperatively to solve the problem.

PBL has been used in virtually every subject area and grade level, up through adult learning situations (Levstik & Barton, 2001; Marx, Blumenfeld, Krajcik, & Soloway, 1997; Scott, 1994). However, overall, PBL has been implemented more often in science and mathematics, and many of the instructional examples one finds involve one or both of those curricular areas (Fortus, Krajcikb, Dershimerb, Marx, & Mamlok-Naamand, 2005; Satchwell & Loepp, 2003).

Because PBL increases motivation to learn, teamwork, and collaborative skills, it is now recommended as a 21st-century teaching technique (Cole & Wasburn-Moses, 2010; Partnership for 21st Century Skills, 2004, 2009). In fact, some proponents of project-based learning view modern instructional technologies and communications/networking technologies as essential in project-based learning (Boss & Krauss, 2007). An excellent pair of brief introductory videos on PBL is available at the website www.edutopia.org/project-based-learning, and the first of those videos is strongly recommended as a quick introduction to PBL.

Of course, through the years, many other terms have been used for this instructional approach, including *problem-based learning, inquiry learning, authentic learning,* and *discovery learning.* However, the general instructional approach remains the same: students identifying and seeking to solve real-world problems that they consider important and developing various projects (sometimes called "artifacts") that may be used to demonstrate their knowledge and communicate their problem solution to others (Bender & Crane, 2011; Fleischner & Manheimer, 1997; Knowlton, 2003; Marzano, 2007).

As various proponents of PBL have described different types of projects for different grade levels, a PBL language has arisen within the educational literature. While different proponents of PBL use these terms in slightly different ways, an understanding of this terminology will help teachers understand the basis of PBL as an instructional approach. Box 1.1 presents several of these commonly used terms and their definitions, and as teachers move into PBL applications, they will need to understand these terms.

Box 1.1 The Lingo of PBL

Anchor. This is the basis for posing a question. An anchor serves to ground the instruction in a real-world scenario, and it might be a newspaper article, an interesting video, a problem posed by a political or advocacy group, or a multimedia presentation designed to "set the stage" for the project (Cognition and Technology Group at Vanderbilt, 1992a, 1992b; Grant, 2010).

Artifacts. Items created within the course of a project that represent possible solutions to the problem or aspects of the solution to the problem. The term *artifact* is used in order to emphasize that not all projects result in a written report or a presentation. Artifacts might include these, but they might also include digital videos, portfolios, podcasts, websites, poems, songs, or chants that illustrate content; art projects resulting from the project; role-play scenarios or one-act plays that represent problem solutions; newspaper articles for school or local newspapers; reports presented orally to various government bodies or other organizations; and recommendations or guidelines for actions on certain issues. In short, an artifact may be virtually anything that the project requires, given the overall expectation that the artifacts represent things required by and used in the real world (Grant, 2010). Also, in most PBL instruction, there is a heavy emphasis on 21st-century skills, so many artifacts do involve development or creation using modern digital technologies.

Authentic achievement. Represents the emphasis that the learning stemming from these projects should stem from real-world scenarios and represent the types of things adults might be expected to do in the real world (Barell, 2007).

Brainstorming. The brainstorming process students undergo to formulate a plan for project tasks is similar to other brainstorming activities, in that the goal is to get down as many ideas for possible task solution as possible, without ruling out any ideas initially. In many cases, this process needs to be directly taught to students, since some students will immediately find problems in the ideas of others, unless specifically instructed in the brainstorming process (Grant, 2010).

(Continued)

Box 1.1 (Continued)

Driving question. The primary question that provides the overall task or stated goal for the PBL project. This should be specifically stated to be highly motivational; something that the students might find meaningful and feel passionately about (Grant, 2010; Larmer & Mergendoller, 2010).

Expeditionary learning. Expeditionary learning is one form of project-based learning that involves taking actual trips or expeditions to various locations in the community related to the project itself. In the sample project presented later in this chapter, an expedition might be taken to the actual plantation, the setting for the cedar tree harvest, in order to actually obtain a count of cedar trees that will allow completion of the project. Alternatively, the sample project could be accomplished without such an expedition, which would represent a more typical PBL experience. In fact, teachers should note that the vast majority of PBL examples are not expeditionary learning projects.

Student voice and choice. This phrase is used to represent the fact that students should have some say (some proponents of PBL would say exclusive say) in project selection and statement of the essential question (Larmer & Mergendoller, 2010).

Web 2.0. The term *web 2.0* has recently been used to represent the fact that technology-based instruction has moved far beyond merely accessing information using the Internet (Ferriter & Garry, 2010). Rather, web 2.0 tools stress the fact that students, working collaboratively in modern instructional technology environments, are actually creating knowledge rather than merely using technology to passively gain knowledge. Thus, web 2.0 is not a collection of new technology applications but, rather, a way of using current applications to help students solve problems and become contributors to knowledge.

As this PBL language suggests, there are many common elements to PBL projects. First, while the project assignments themselves vary considerably, nearly all PBL projects are focused on authentic problems or issues from the real world (Larmer & Mergendoller, 2010). This focus on authentic learning experiences that students might well be required to accomplish in the real world is a hallmark of virtually all PBL experiences and typically increases students' motivations to actively participate in the projects.

Next, most PBL assignments require extensive collaborative work (Grant, 2010). Students have to collaboratively plan their team's actions as they move toward problem solution, by developing a plan of action and beginning to develop a description or guidelines for development of their products or artifacts (Larmer & Mergendoller, 2010). Research and development of those products or artifacts may take many days and typically involves the creation of multimedia presentations, hands-on demonstrations, perhaps a working model, a portfolio, a podcast, digital videos, or a test model for the project or problem (Cote, 2007; Land & Green, 2000; Partnership for 21st Century Skills, 2004, 2009). PBL projects might be focused toward only one subject, or they might be interdisciplinary. The sample PBL project that follows illustrates these aspects of PBL.

> PBL projects might be focused toward only one subject, or they might be interdisciplinary.

A Sample PBL Project

A PBL project dealing with harvesting a specific type of wood for furniture production is presented in Box 1.2. This project is a relatively simple one that would be appropriate for a variety of upper elementary and middle school classes, including science, ecology, and perhaps mathematics, or in a combination of those classes, as an interdisciplinary project facilitated by several teachers. This example is very basic in the sense that much more technology can be, and typically is, incorporated into most PBL projects. Also, most projects involve longer time frames than does this example. Still, this does demonstrate many aspects of what any simple PBL project might involve, and it serves to illustrate that, even in educational environments that are not rich in technology, PBL provides a viable, dynamic instructional option.

Box 1.2 PBL Project Example: Cedar Tree Harvest

Anchor: How Many Cedar Trees Can We Harvest?

A plantation home in Virginia, the Cedar Plantation, is owned by the descendents of the family that originally owned the plantation home but is operated as a state historic site in conjunction with the State of Virginia. The family wants to allow a family-owned furniture company to harvest a selected allotment of white and red cedar trees each year for furniture

(Continued)

Box 1.2 (Continued)

production. On this plantation property, cedar trees occupy all of the 49 acres of woods, but the family is not sure how many trees are on the property, and they want to be assured that selected harvesting does not deplete their entire supply of cedar trees. Of the 49-acre property, approximately 12 acres, give or take, are visible from the plantation. Also, approximately 21 acres are believed to be swampland, but all of the low-lying land is on the distant side of the woods that is not visible from the house.

The family invited a fifth-grade class at the local middle school to undertake a project to determine how many trees might be selectively harvested each year, on an acre-by-acre basis. The family wants to harvest no more than 50 percent of the cedar trees in any given year, and they instructed the class to use the following data in their project, based on growth norms.

The teacher and the students discussed this project and decided to undertake it using three teams of students working independently in the classroom. Together, the teacher and the students decided that each of the three teams would devote a minimum of 20 hours to this project, spending a minimum of 30 minutes on this project daily in either their science or mathematics class. Of course, on some days, the class will spend up to an hour on this work.

Information on Cedar Growth and Family Guidelines

From seedling to maturity	Takes approximately 45 years
Average number of mature red cedars per acre	53 (based on cedar count on only one acre of the higher-ground property)
Average number of mature white cedars per acre	48 (based on cedar count on only one acre of the low-lying swampland on the property)

Tasks to Be Accomplished

Students will work in groups to accomplish several tasks:

1. Classify the types of cedar trees on the plantation. For the most part, white cedars grow in the lower-land swamps on the plantation, whereas red cedars grow on the higher ground.

(Continued)

Box 1.2 (Continued)

Verify the average number of trees on each acre and the total number owned by the plantation. A webquest will be completed to guide the research on cedar tree growth in various terrains, and all students are expected to complete that webquest, either working individually or in pairs. The family requested, if possible, an actual count of trees on at least four additional acres, scattered across the property in order to accurately extrapolate the number of cedar trees (completing this task will change this from a PBL example to an expeditionary-learning PBL example). These data on the extrapolated cedar tree count should be summarized on a spreadsheet.

2. Determine the life span for cedar trees in upstate Virginia to ascertain how many trees naturally expire in a given year. If possible, provide some guidance on "worst case" scenarios (e.g., a two-year drought, late snowfall that kills new-growth seedlings in a given year) that might limit the number of trees that should be harvested yearly. Determine the number of trees available for harvest each year, based on average tree count on the four acres and other guidelines.

3. Determine a reasonable plan for selective harvest of the cedar trees that will not deplete any single section of the woodlands and will not negatively impact the view of the cedar woodlands from the plantation house itself.

4. Create a multimedia presentation that will persuade all family members of the viability of cedar harvests and the negligible impact such harvests will have on the view of the plantation from the plantation home itself.

Students Will Need Access to the Following:

1. A field trip opportunity to visit the plantation and count trees for the project

2. Computers with Microsoft Office, PowerPoint, Excel or another spreadsheet, videos, and cameras

3. Websites with information on cedar trees, anticipated drought conditions in Virginia, etc.

4. Topological map of Western Virginia to accurately determine how many acres of swampland might exist on the plantation

(Continued)

Box 1.2 (Continued)

Anticipated Artifacts

1. Four brief reports addressing questions within the project

2. PowerPoint or video presentation(s) summarizing the reported information, either for each individual question or for the questions together. This must include sufficient detail to be convincing.

3. Specific guidelines for harvesting recommendations

In undertaking the PBL project, students in the class might be divided into two or three teams with each team responsible for addressing the problem overall as well as generating the required artifacts to complete the project. In this and most PBL projects, there might be a variety of acceptable solutions to the problem, and it should be expected that various teams of students will come up with different solutions. For example, because some family members in this example are clearly concerned with the woodland view from the plantation house, one group of students might recommend that the several acres of woodland that can be seen directly from the plantation house be eliminated from the cedar tree harvest, and that would be a perfectly acceptable solution. However, another group might allow harvesting of large cedar trees up to within 100 feet of the viewable tree line, while restricting the harvest of smaller trees. That would be another acceptable solution that would result in a different number of trees available for harvest as well as different guidelines on the number of trees that could be harvested annually. Also, the average count of red cedars and white cedars on the plantation might vary, depending on how one defined swampland and each group's interpretation of topological maps of the area. Again, multiple answers are not only possible but quite likely for this project.

For that reason, rubrics are frequently used to provide some structure to the PBL instructional experience, as well as to evaluate various artifacts in the classroom. Rubrics should be comprehensive enough to suggest the level of detail desired in any possible problem solution, as well as identify specific types of issues that the teams should consider. Also, these rubrics should be shared with and emphasized for the students as the basis for what is anticipated (Boss & Krauss, 2007). A sample rubric for use with this particular project is presented in Box 1.3.

> Rubrics are frequently used to provide some structure to the PBL instructional experience, as well as to evaluate various artifacts in the classroom.

Box 1.3 Rubric for Evaluating the Cedar Tree Harvest Project

Stated Objective	1	2	3	4
Team compiled data on red and white cedar trees per acre, using a spreadsheet.	Team achieved an average tree count for each tree type but failed to compile data on a suitable spreadsheet.	Team gathered and compiled data for each type of cedar. Team compiled data in a spreadsheet with minimal organization and no recommendations on different types of cedars on different types of land.	Team gathered and compiled data for each type of cedar, included recommendations for different cedars on different land types, and created a spreadsheet.	Team gathered and compiled data for each type of cedar, including more than minimal recommendations on different cedars and land types, and created a spreadsheet that was organized, well labeled, color coded, and easy to interpret.
Team determined an average life span for red and white cedars in two types of environments.	Team did not use an appropriate procedure for calculating normal life span for red and white cedars in VA.	Team used an appropriate procedure for each type of cedar but came up with incorrect answers.	Team used an appropriate procedure and came up with accurate data on average life span for each type of cedar.	Team used an appropriate procedure for calculating normal life span for each type of cedar tree, provided accurate data on averages, and generated different recommendations for different land types.

(Continued)

Box 1.3 (Continued)

Stated Objective	1	2	3	4
Team developed a recommended number of trees that might be harvested yearly.	Team's recommendation was not sufficiently detailed or justified.	Team's recommendation was adequate but was not well organized or justified.	Team had a reasonable number and an appropriately detailed justification for their recommended harvest number.	Team developed a reasonable recommendation that was detailed and well justified, with different recommendations for different cedars and land types.
Team presented multimedia presentation(s) that persuaded family members to allow the harvest.	Presentation only integrated one type of technology and was not convincing.	Presentation integrated two technologies and was persuasive but not personal enough to incite action.	Presentation included worst-case scenarios with a minimum of two technologies but was not completely convincing.	Presentation integrated three or more technologies, including different recommendations for different land types and different cedar trees.

Evaluation Procedure: Student scores may range from four to sixteen. Either the teacher or a group of students working collaboratively with the teacher awards points to groups of students for each of the objectives listed and then totals those points. Point totals of 15–16 equate to an A on the project. A total of 13–14 equals a B; 10–12 equates to a C, and less than 10 indicates a need to redo the project.

In this rubric, the teacher or teachers have clearly established some indicators about the level of detail necessary for the project solution. In the rubric itself, indicators suggest that students should consider average life spans for different types of cedar trees and document their deliberations relative to that question. Different assumptions made by different student teams will impact the ultimate recommendations for the tree harvest. Of course, information on these issues must be researched by the students, and such research for many PBL projects involves an active and informed use of the Internet.

With this noted, rubrics should certainly not be the only type of instructional or evaluation guidance that teachers will provide. In fact, a wide variety of instructional practices may be built into a PBL project, depending on the depth, level, and time limitations of the project. For example, one or more webquests are frequently incorporated into PBL projects in order to provide some structure for the assignment and assist students in researching the information they will need to solve their problem. An example of a webquest that would assist in this particular PBL assignment is presented in Box 1.4. Some proponents of PBL have suggested that a webquest itself is an example of PBL instruction (Grant, 2010). In most cases, however, webquests are considered a means of assisting in research or perhaps as one artifact resulting from the project.

Box 1.4 Webquest on Expected Tree Life Span

Objectives

1. Identify the expected life span for cedar trees to use in calculations on cedar tree harvest

2. Find out the prevalence of the most common diseases of cedar trees and determine if those data need to be included in the estimate for the cedar tree harvest

Activities

1. Obtain information on life span of red and white cedars. Write a two-paragraph summary on the life span of cedar trees on the plantation. Of course, many times several different answers can be found using different information sources. Try the following URLs and see if they agree. For each website, make a note of the answer and note whether it represents average life span or maximum life span.

(Continued)

Box 1.4 (Continued)

- Wiki.answers.com/Q/What_is_the_lifespan_of_a_
cedar_tree
- Factoz.com/cedar-trees-lifespan
- www.rook.org/earl/bwca/nature/trees/thujaocc.html

2. Can various types of cedar trees account for these discrepancies? You will need to determine what percentage of trees is white cedar versus red cedar on the cedar plantation.

3. The team must devise a reasonable procedure for determining how they resolved discrepancies in life span for red and white cedar trees and explain that in detail in a two- to four-paragraph statement. This will become part of your final presentation.

4. Are there diseases that must be factored into the question? Check on diseases for cedar trees in Virginia at the following website. Write a paragraph to explain why you did or did not include this factor in your overall recommendation for the cedar tree harvest.

- www.gardensalive.com/article.asp?ai=879&bhcd2=
1295464860

5. The team must make a determination as to what an "adult" cedar tree is (this should be described in terms of how many feet tall the tree is). The team will also need to calculate growth rates to determine how long a cedar tree takes to reach adult status. This should be summarized in a written paragraph. The following website will help:

- www.cedartrees.com/our_trees.asp

Some proponents of PBL have suggested that a webquest itself is an example of PBL instruction. In most cases, however, webquests are considered a means of assisting in research or perhaps as one artifact resulting from the project.

In addition to this sample project, teachers should investigate other projects, and many are available on the Internet as well as throughout this text. Box 1.5 presents a list of websites that provide information or sample PBL projects that teachers might review, as well as information on how to plan a PBL project.

Box 1.5 Websites on Project-Based Learning

Bie.org. This is the home website for the Buck Institute for Education, which is a nonprofit corporation dedicated to project-based learning. This site can offer materials for purchase in PBL as well as professional development opportunities for project-based learning.

Edutopia.org/project-based-learning. This site is provided by the George Lucas Educational Foundation and offers several short videos including a three-minute video, *Introduction to Project-Based Learning,* and a nine-minute video, *Project-Based Learning: An Overview.* These are recommended as excellent introductions to PBL. One can also join the new online magazine focusing on project-based learning.

Imet.csus.edu/imet2/stanfillj/workshops/pbl/description.htm. This site is perhaps the single richest resource on project-based learning, in that many other sites are linked. One can find many examples of PBL projects and information on how projects may be designed and implemented.

Internet4classrooms.com/project.htm. This site provides a compendium of other links that can support project-based learning. Examples include a site of biographies of famous persons in a variety of areas (science, history, politics), as well as sites providing statistics on various countries. This site should be provided as a resource directly to students in many middle and high school PBL projects.

PBL-online.org. This is a site related to the Buck Institute that provides information on how to design PBL projects using five sequenced tasks: begin with the end in mind, craft the driving question, plan the assessment, map the project, and manage the process. Various video examples of teachers collaboratively planning to implement PBL projects are provided as a professional development source on PBL.

Superkids.com. This website identifies educational software for students, listing almost 200 examples of problem-solving software for the classroom. Ratings of this software by students, parents, and experts allow teachers to select programs that might be appropriate for their classroom.

(Continued)

Box 1.5 (Continued)

ThinkQuest.org. This website provides a platform, referred to as ThinkQuest, that teachers use in constructing PBL projects for their classroom. ThinkQuest is a protected online environment that enables teachers to design and carry out learning projects within the classroom or in conjunction with other teachers worldwide in the ThinkQuest global community. On this website, teachers can find links to more than 7,000 project ideas and activities for PBL.

Components of PBL Assignments

Nearly all teachers have required students to complete a wide variety of projects over the years, but proponents of the PBL instructional approach indicate that not all projects done in classrooms should be considered examples of PBL (Grant, 2010; Larmer & Mergendoller, 2010). For example, as indicated by Larmer and Mergendoller (2010), students must perceive the PBL project as personally meaningful to them in order to realize their maximum involvement in solving the problem, and those authors consider that to be a defining characteristic of PBL versus other projects undertaken in schools. Other proponents of PBL emphasize other aspects of PBL as defining characteristics, such as specification of student roles within the context of the project (Barell, 2007) or a driving, highly motivating question that is authentic by virtue of being focused on real-world scenarios (Grant, 2010). In fact, most descriptions of PBL identify a variety of specific components or specific types of activities that should be included in order for a project to be considered an example of PBL (Barell, 2007; Baron, 2011; Grant, 2010; Larmer & Mergendoller, 2010).

> Most descriptions of PBL identify a variety of specific components or specific types of activities that should be included in order for a project to be considered an example of PBL.

Nearly all descriptions of PBL suggest that teachers, working in collaboration with students, develop a highly motivating, guiding question that the students will relate to (Barell, 2007; Grant, 2010). This is sometimes referred to as the "driving question" for the PBL experience. In PBL, students are given or develop a challenging, complex task that resembles tasks adults might face in the real world. In most projects, such a driving question will not have a simple solution

(Grant, 2010), and various acceptable solutions are likely to be generated by the different groups working on the project. Next, students might be provided with an "anchor" that may be an introductory video, narrative, or presentation that indicates the importance of the driving question and suggests why and how the problem might be addressed.

Once an anchor is provided, and a guiding question, problem, or project is determined, students working together will engage in a complex series of tasks to plan and organize their activities in order to move toward a solution to the problem (Grant, 2010; Larmer & Mergendoller, 2010). These tasks vary from one proponent of PBL to another, but they generally include the following:

- Brainstorming possible problem solutions,
- Identifying a specific series of topics to help collect information,
- Dividing up responsibilities for information gathering,
- Developing a time line for information gathering,
- Searching for information on the problem or question,
- Synthesizing the data collected,
- Collaborative decision making on how to move forward from that point,
- Determination of what additional information might be essential, and
- Developing a product, or multiple products or artifacts, that allows students to communicate the results of their work.

As this list of tasks indicates, PBL projects can be quite extensive and may involve a variety of time frames (Fleischner & Manheimer, 1997; Knowlton, 2003). Given the wide variation of descriptions of PBL instructional experiences, Chapter 3 of this text will describe the various components of PBL more comprehensively, as well as provide guidance for development and design of PBL projects.

> In PBL, students are given or develop a challenging, complex task that resembles tasks adults might face in the real world.

Rationale for a PBL Instructional Approach

In the same way that various proponents of PBL emphasize different components of this instructional approach, various advocates identify different reasons for employing this teaching using this framework. Some advocates have focused on increased levels of student engagement with the subject matter or higher levels of motivation to complete assignments that are personally meaningful to the students (Drake & Long, 2009; Fleischner & Manheimer, 1997; Grant, 2010).

In contrast, others suggest that PBL instruction is more likely to prepare students with 21st-century technology and problem-solving skills (Bender & Crane, 2011; Partnership for 21st Century Skills, 2007, 2009). Finally, the social learning basis for this instructional approach is cited as an advantage by virtually all proponents of PBL (Barell, 2007; Drake & Long, 2009; Grant, 2010). As one example, the Project on the Effectiveness of Project-Based Learning identified three criteria that summarize these aspects of PBL:

1. Curriculum that is built around problems with an emphasis on cognitive skills and knowledge;

2. A student-centered learning environment that utilizes small groups and active learning where teachers serve as facilitators, and

3. Student outcomes focused on the development of skills, motivation, and a love for life-long learning (Drake & Long, 2009).

> PBL instruction is more likely to prepare students with 21st-century technology and problem-solving skills.

The PBL approach encourages students to participate in project planning, research, investigation, and the application of new knowledge in order to reach a solution to their problem (Rule & Barrera, 2008). In that sense, PBL is rather like problems confronted in life in that frequently there is no apparent organized structure that allows one to reach a solution, and that structure must be created and imposed by the students themselves in PBL. This type of learning forces students, working in collaborative teams, to create meaning from the chaos of a plethora of information, in order to articulate and effectively present a solution to the problem (Rhem, 1998).

> In an age of instant communication with today's digital media, and availability of nearly unlimited information on the Internet, advocates of PBL suggest that making sense of the virtual mountain of chaotic information is exactly the type of knowledge construction that every student in today's world needs to master.

Of course, in an age of instant communication with today's digital media, and availability of nearly unlimited information on the Internet, advocates of PBL suggest that making sense of the virtual mountain of chaotic information is exactly the type of knowledge construction that every student in today's world needs to master (Barell, 2010; Partnership for 21st Century Skills, 2007, 2009). Further, the integration of assorted subject areas with various thinking skills in PBL helps teachers work through extensive content standards by teaching students to see the connectedness of the big ideas within the various curriculum areas (Rule & Barrera, 2008).

Project-Based Learning and Differentiated Instruction

Many proponents of PBL suggest that project-based instruction provides wonderful opportunities for differentiating instruction in most public school classes (Bender & Crane, 2011; O'Meara, 2010; Schlemmer & Schlemmer, 2008; Tomlinson, 2010; Tomlinson, Brimijoin, & Narvaez, 2008). For example, in Barell's (2007) description of PBL, he described how PBL projects can be improved by focusing on the content to be learned, the instructional/learning process, and the instructional products that demonstrate learning, and these three factors are likewise the major focal points of Tomlinson's description of differentiated instruction (Tomlinson, 1999, 2010; Tomlinson et al., 2008). In the chapters to follow, these three factors will repeatedly appear as important considerations in planning and conducting PBL projects, and this demonstrates the relationship between project-based learning and differentiated instruction, both of which are viewed today as examples of 21st-century instruction (Barell, 2010; Tomlinson, 2010).

> Three factors, learning content standards, learning processes, and products of learning, are the major focal points of both PBL and of differentiated instruction.

More pointedly, in order to meet the needs of diverse learners in today's classrooms, a variety of instructional activities are needed, with some students completing some activities while other students complete others. This is both the essence of differentiated instruction as well as the overall result of PBL-based instruction. In that sense, PBL does tend to foster high levels of differentiated instruction in most instances.

A Plant Growth PBL Project for Grade 3

Of course, the level of differentiation can depend on the length of time devoted to the PBL project, and not all PBL projects are as extensive as the project presented in Box 1.2. Indeed, some projects may be completed without leaving the classroom, and these may take only one or a few periods or portions of instructional periods to complete. Imagine, for example, a teacher in a third-grade classroom involved in a study of the life cycle of plants. That teacher might create cooperative learning groups in which each group was responsible for a presentation on one stage of that life cycle (seedling, early growth, flowering and reseeding, etc.) with the overall goal of presenting some information to the class on that particular phase of plant development (more on this type of cooperative learning is presented in Chapter 4). That type of PBL project might take only one or two periods for research, with an additional period for presentation of the information. A project description for this work is presented in Box 1.6.

Box 1.6 Plant Growth PBL Project

A Primary PBL Example

Anchor: How Do Plants Grow?

The third-grade classes in our primary school are presenting a one-hour assembly for all of the classes from kindergarten up through Grade 3 to celebrate the coming spring season. Various classes will study different aspects of the season, and our class will need to present a 15-minute demonstration on how plants grow in the spring during that assembly. A video of the entire assembly, including our presentation, will be made available on the school website for all of our parents and the community.

Driving Questions: Information We Need to Find

How can we present the life of a plant and the importance of the changes that take place in the spring?

Tasks to Be Accomplished

Students will work in groups together to accomplish several tasks:

1. Identify and describe the stages of plant life. How many are there? How are these stages of life defined?

(Continued)

Box 1.6 (Continued)

2. What do plants look like in various stages? Obtain pictures of videos showing the stages.

3. What is happening in various stages? How can we show that?

Students Will Need Access to the Following:

1. Computers with Microsoft Office, PowerPoint, Excel or another spreadsheet, videos, and cameras

2. Websites with information on plant life

Anticipated Artifacts

1. A one-page summary of each stage of the plant's life cycle, complete with pictures or video showing that stage

2. A time-lapse video of plant growth (obtain from Internet, if possible)

3. An organized presentation including PowerPoint or video presentation(s) summarizing the stages of plant life

In order to differentiate instruction within that project, the teacher might create a heterogeneous group for differentiated activities, with each group including a strong reader, a strong writer, a technology-savvy student (who could find Internet examples of plant life cycles), a weaker reader, and a fairly well organized student leader. In that manner, each member in the group would be able to use their own personal strengths to achieve the group goal while also learning from the rest of the group.

As this example illustrates, project-based learning can be considered as a vehicle for providing highly differentiated instruction in virtually any classroom. Box 1.7 presents several other examples of shorter-term and longer-term projects in which a teacher might easily develop and incorporate various differentiated activities.

> In order to differentiate instruction within that project, the teacher might create a heterogeneous group for differentiated activities, with each group including a strong reader, a strong writer, a technology-savvy student (who could find Internet examples of plant life cycles), a weaker reader, and a fairly well organized student leader.

Box 1.7 Examples of Differentiation in PBL Conclusions

A. In the PBL project previously described (harvesting cedar trees in an ecologically sound fashion), students needing enrichment might be required to create and edit a podcast on various life span differences between assorted types of cedars or disease scenarios that impact tree growth and harvesting. That type of assignment would require a storyboard for the podcast, and students with strong writing skills would certainly have an opportunity to show their skills in that area. Others could participate in the podcast creation through camera work, editing, or the provision of props for the podcast's Internet-based content. Students needing intervention and remediation in various reading or research skills might be required to create or participate in a blog on forest growth as one part of their responsibilities, and the somewhat shorter format used in most blogs would provide a chance for struggling students to practice their writing skills without the intimidation factor associated with longer written projects.

B. Many projects can be differentiated to specifically address the needs and abilities of musical learners, bodily kinesthetic learners, and learners with other strengths. If a fourth-grade teacher is undertaking a project on the types of life within the oceans of the world, that teacher might begin by summarizing the main 10 or 12 points within the project content. These may be definitions of the various types of sea creatures—crustaceans, fishes, mammals, etc.—or points that emphasize the differences and relationships among them (e.g., predators/prey, common characteristics). In fact, teachers might even form small groups and let those groups determine what those critical 10 or 12 points might be, while providing some coaching and guidance along the way. Then students with musical ability might be tasked to create some form of chant or song to teach those main concepts. Alternatively, students who learn best by bodily movement might be asked to develop a "movement model" that could show the relationships among planets, asteroids, moons, stars, galactic dust, etc. All of these could be identified as different artifacts that are required within a PBL project.

(Continued)

Box 1.7 (Continued)

C. In a kindergarten PBL project, students might undertake the study of living and nonliving things in the schoolyard. Teams of students could be formed to collect either actual examples of various objects in the schoolyard (grass, leaves, paper, or trash) or pictures of those objects (swing sets, baseball bases, etc.). Students might then work in teams to identify and describe differences among these classes of objects. To differentiate this assignment, the linguistic learners, who are more likely to be academically accomplished writers, can write down a sentence about each object noting the differences. Subsequently, interpersonally skilled learners might be used to actually present the team results to the class, and during that presentation, bodily kinesthetic learners might participate by holding up the objects and pictures of objects being described.

D. Biology students in high school might undertake this project: identifying infectious bacteria within our school. In developing that project idea, the use of microscopes would be essential, and bodily kinesthetic learners would benefit from the hands-on nature of the project. Brainstorming various locations for such bacteria would be useful (though the teacher might wish to disallow study of bacteria on commodes!). However, collecting bacteria samples on classroom desks, doorknobs, floors, lockers, kitchen and bathroom sinks, etc. would be acceptable. Students with linguistic skills could write summaries, and students with mathematical or classification skills might develop spreadsheets to depict bacteria in various locations.

E. Students in middle school or high school who are involved in a mathematics class, or perhaps a consumer economics class, might undertake a project answering this question: Can our family purchase a new car for me? One can imagine how pressing that question might be! Students would then need to account for their parents' income (both Dad's and Mom's salary or some income figures created by the teacher as an example), any monthly part-time work income that the student might generate, and other family income such as child support or tax refunds.

(Continued)

Box 1.7 (Continued)

They would also need information on bills that must be paid (monthly and yearly bills, info on insurance rates for adolescents, car costs for used automobiles). By compiling all of those data, students would get a good sense of the family budgeting process. If parents are reluctant to share the actual family budget information, the teacher might create a family and provide these data in some form.

F. An example of an upper elementary project in health might involve a survey of our food! Students could develop a presentation for the school administration on the types of breakfast and lunch meals served in the school cafeteria, as compared to the recently published "Food Groups Plate" graphic that was developed in 2011 by the Department of Health and Human Services of the federal government. In comparison with that representation of appropriate food groups, do the meals served in the cafeteria adequately represent the governmental recommended diet?

This chapter has presented a rationale for PBL in the context of 21st-century instruction. While teachers have presented various instructional project assignments to their students for many decades, the move to PBL involves much more than merely the assignment of an individual project within a given instructional unit. Rather, PBL involves a shift to student-centered learning on authentic, engaging problems and questions, and the increased use of web 2.0 tools and other instructional technologies in the teaching process. The next chapter presents a discussion of PBL in the classroom and research supportive of PBL.

2

Project-Based Learning in the Classroom

Making PBL Work in the Classroom

As the discussion in Chapter 1 makes clear, PBL does involve a different approach to instruction when compared to the traditional classroom, and teachers will need to explore many questions prior to becoming comfortable in trying PBL. First, teachers should consider how PBL differs from projects they may have done previously. Next, teachers will need to consider various ways that PBL fits within their instructional practices and how those practices may be modified as they move into PBL. Finally, in today's educational environment, all instructional practices must be supported by research, and teachers should have some general awareness of the research basis for PBL.

PBL Versus a Traditional Project Assignment

In considering the use of PBL as an instructional approach, teachers must first understand the basic differences between PBL projects and the types of instructional projects that have characterized educational endeavors for many decades (Boss & Krauss, 2007; Larmer &

Mergendoller, 2010). As one example, imagine a social studies teacher in middle school who initiates an instructional unit on the American Revolution. That teacher might well assign a project within that instructional unit involving the following assignment.

> *Every student will create a poster or art project depicting several causes of the American Revolution and the relationship of those causes to the Declaration of Independence and the previous and subsequent battles within the American Revolution. Content should reflect all or most of the following points: Sugar Act of 1764, Stamp Act of 1765, Boston Massacre of 1770, Tea Act and Boston Tea Party of 1773, Battle at Lexington/ Concord of 1775, Battle of Bunker Hill of 1775, and the Declaration of Independence of 1776.*

This traditional type of project assignment has many advantages, and for that reason, this type of project has frequently been assigned in all core U.S. history classes for many years. Such projects are typically done as either homework or a combination of class work and homework and tend to fit within a single instructional unit on the American Revolution. These types of projects can represent the conceptual connections between singular events in that unit and help students understand the concepts and big ideas within the curriculum. In completing this type of project, students would have to access information on the causes of the American Revolution, the Declaration of Independence, and the initial battles of the revolution. They could then do a diagram or "concept map" type of poster relating those causes to the Continental Congress and battles of Lexington/Concord and Bunker Hill, which took place prior to the. signing of the Declaration of Independence.

Rather than developing a diagram, another student might choose to develop a pictorial representation showing this content. For example, members of the Continental Congress might be portrayed holding up various papers including copies of previous taxes (e.g., the Sugar Act, the Stamp Act, and the Tea Act), while others might hold up newspapers with headlines about battles fought prior to the Declaration of Independence. In the front of the room, various members signing the Declaration of Independence could be portrayed, and that art project would thus show the big ideas, causes, and time frame of those events.

In short, this type of individual project is perfectly acceptable as an instructional assignment and could be completed in a variety of ways by various students as just described. This is a content-rich instructional project assignment, and it is likely to facilitate learning of the big ideas, underlying concepts, relationships, and specific content within that topic.

However, in spite of those advantages, this would not typically be considered an example of PBL. In fact, there are many distinctions between this project assignment on the American Revolution and PBL instructional approaches that might cover the same content (Cote, 2007; Larmer & Mergendoller, 2010). These would include, at a minimum, the framing of a driving question for the study, student voice and choice inherent in PBL approaches, the collaborative nature of PBL assignments, the longer time frame for PBL projects, the depth of content covered by PBL projects versus traditional project assignments, and the ultimate publication of the results of the students' study efforts.

> Not all content-rich instructional project assignments, even ones that are likely to facilitate learning of specific content, can be considered examples of PBL.

In order to understand these critical distinctions between traditional project assignments in content classes and the PBL instructional approach, various authors have developed lists of common features or essential characteristics of PBL instruction (Barell, 2007, 2010; Cote, 2007; Grant, 2010; Larmer & Mergendoller, 2010). These should not be viewed as steps within the design or instructional process but, rather, as characteristics that should be found in all or most PBL projects. While these vary somewhat from one author to the next, a discussion of these common features can illuminate the level and depth of planning required in PBL instruction. A synthesis of these common features is presented in Box 2.1, and each of these is discussed at length in Chapter 3.

Box 2.1 Essential Characteristics of PBL

Anchor. An introduction and background information to set the stage and generate interest.

Collaborative teamwork. Collaborative teamwork is critical in PBL experiences and is emphasized by every proponent of PBL as one way to make learning experiences more authentic.

Driving question. The driving question should both engage students' attention and focus their efforts.

Feedback and revision. Scaffolded assistance should be routinely provided either by the teacher or within the collaborative instructional process. Feedback can be based on either teacher or peer evaluations.

(Continued)

> ## Box 2.1 (Continued)
>
> *Inquiry and innovation.* Within the broader driving question, the group will need to generate additional questions focused more specifically on project tasks.
>
> *Opportunities for reflection.* Creating opportunities for student reflection within various projects is stressed by all proponents of PBL.
>
> *Process of investigation.* Guidelines for project completion and artifact generation can be used to frame the project. The group may also develop time lines and specific goals for completion of various aspects of the project.
>
> *Publicly presented product.* PBL projects are intended to be authentic examples of the types of problems students confront in the real world, so some public presentation of project results is a critical emphasis within PBL.
>
> *Student voice and choice.* Students should have a voice in some aspects of how the project might be undertaken and be encouraged to exercise choices throughout.

How Does PBL Fit Into the Curriculum?

The first decision teachers must make involves how PBL fits within the curriculum. Is a PBL project going to be an adjunct to one or more instructional units, or is the PBL project intended to serve as a replacement for unit-based instruction for some period of time? Teachers may feel more comfortable moving into PBL-based instruction when PBL assignments are adjuncts to one or more units of instruction within their curriculum, since this is more similar to what teachers have been doing in the classroom. In this case, where the PBL project is intended as an adjunct to the ongoing unit-based instruction, the teacher must determine which instructional standards from one or several contiguous units might be best addressed in the context of the PBL assignments. Again, teachers have always done various projects in most areas of the school curricula, so this type of mapping of curricular standards onto PBL assignments will be nothing new for most of them.

However, many proponents of PBL suggest that PBL should, indeed, replace unit-based instruction entirely (Barell, 2010; Boss & Krauss, 2007; Larmer & Mergendoller, 2010). In this case, educators must carefully consider all of the specific curricular standards that will be taught exclusively through the PBL experience and make certain that each is addressed in some fashion. Teachers can then develop or design specific artifacts that will require students to study, and ultimately master, those curricular standards.

> Many proponents of PBL suggest that PBL should replace unit-based instruction entirely.

Research on the Efficacy of PBL

Teachers today must understand how the instructional approaches they implement are based in research, and in the implementation of PBL, teachers may rest assured that research has consistently shown that PBL is highly effective (Gijbels et al., 2005; Grant, 2010; Partnership for 21st Century Skills, 2009; Thomas, 2000; Walker & Leary, 2008). While this chapter does not provide a complete compendium of research on PBL, the basic research results are discussed herein.

Two advantages of PBL seem to stand out more prominently in the research. First, PBL increases students' motivation and interest in completing the work that is required (Barell, 2010; Belland et al., 2009; Blumenfeld et al., 1991; Fortus et al., 2005; Grant, 2010; Tassinari, 1996; Walker & Leary, 2008; Worthy, 2000). As indicated in the discussion in Chapter 1, the anchor and driving questions used to frame PBL projects typically involve real-world scenarios, and this emphasis tends to make instruction more relevant to students' lives. This factor, coupled with student choice in various activities, tends to increase motivation and often results in increased academic engagement.

For example, one study compared PBL to traditional instruction in several fourth-grade classrooms and showed that students participating in PBL had 4.27 more minutes of on-task, engaged science instruction than did the control group for every 45 minutes of science instruction (Drake & Long, 2009). This resulted in 12.80 hours of additional science instruction over the course of the year. Other research has shown improved attitudes toward certain subjects, such as mathematics, when project-based learning was implemented (Boaler, 2002), and this likewise would tend to lead to increased student engagement with the academic content.

> PBL instruction is more relevant to students and increases students' motivation and interest in completing the work that is required.

Second, given this increased engagement with the learning content, research has shown that student achievement increases in project-based learning (Barell, 2007, 2010; Boaler, 2002; Bransford, Brown, & Cocking, 2000; Bransford et al., 1986; Grant, 2010; Mergendoller et al., 2007; Perkins, 1992; Stepien, Gallagher, & Workman, 1992; Strobel & van Barneveld, 2008). One meta-analysis synthesized a large body of research and indicated that students may improve as much as 30 percent in their understanding of concepts as a result of project-based learning (Gijbels et al., 2005). Further, research in a wide variety of subject areas has likewise shown this increase in student achievement as a result of PBL (Scott, 1994; Stepien et al., 1992; Strobel & van Barneveld, 2008; Tassinari, 1996; Walker & Leary, 2008).

> Research has shown that student achievement increases in project-based learning.

With these primary research findings identified, there are also other advantages to project-based learning that have been documented by the research. While a complete compilation of this research is not possible in this context, Box 2.2 presents some of the other positive research-based outcomes of project-based learning.

While the impressive array of research results in Box 2.2 shows that project-based learning is a research-proven instructional

---

Box 2.2 Research on Project-Based Learning

1. PBL meets an often-stated goal of educators by stressing deeper understanding. Research has shown that PBL results in higher levels of conceptual processing, higher understanding of principles, deeper reflection, and increased critical thinking (Boaler, 2002; Bransford et al., 2000; Grant, 2010; Marzano, 2007; Marzano, Pickering, & Pollock, 2001; Strobel & van Barneveld, 2008; Thomas, 2000).

2. PBL results in enhanced retention of information because students are processing information in a distinctly different manner than is typically involved in rote learning (Barell, 2007; Geier et al., 2008; Marzano et al., 2001).

3. PBL results in increased use of effective problem-solving strategies and has been shown to be effective in a wide variety of core academic areas including mathematics, science, economics, and history (Stepien et al., 1992; Strobel & van Barneveld, 2008; Walker & Leary, 2008).

(Continued)

Box 2.2 (Continued)

4. PBL fosters the types of problem-solving skills and deep conceptual skills that are required in the modern work environment of the 21st century (Barell, 2007; Fleischner & Manheimer, 1997; Grant, 2010; Partnership for 21st Century Skills, 2007, 2009; Strobel & van Barneveld, 2008; Thomas, 2000).

5. PBL typically involves extensive use of instructional technology by the students and thus fosters expertise in the types of technology used in the 21st century (Cognition and Technology Group at Vanderbilt, 1992a, 1992b; Hickey et al. & the Cognition and Technology Group at Vanderbilt, 1994).

6. PBL is particularly effective with lower-achieving students, making this an excellent option for differentiating instruction for struggling students (Geier et al., 2008; Mergendoller et al., 2007).

technique, one important research conclusion must be highlighted since it represents a critical concern of teachers today: Does project-based learning result in higher achievement than teaching approaches that maximize content coverage? In order to understand the critical nature of this question, one must understand the incredible pressure that today's teachers are under to cover all of the content standards in the curriculum and, thus, increase students' achievement as measured by today's state-mandated high-stakes tests.

Many states have, as of 2011, adopted the Common Core State Standards (www.corestandards.org/the-standards) in various curriculum areas, and teachers may wonder how PBL fits into the imperative to teach the Common Core (while space prohibits discussion of standards from various states that have not adopted the Common Core State Standards, the appendix in this book discusses PBL in relation to Texas standards, as one example of a state not adopting the Common Core). Because of the strong emphasis on standards-based learning as measured by state assessments, as well as the ever-increasing need to meet higher educational standards, teachers today are understandably quite reluctant to undertake any innovation that does not result in improved academic achievement relative to the educational standards used by their state.

> Teachers today are under incredible pressure to cover all of the content standards in the curriculum and, thus, increase students' achievement as measured by today's state-mandated high-stakes tests, and they wonder how PBL fits into that imperative.

Of course, some proponents of PBL might suggest that, in spite of teachers' concerns, this is not a relevant question. In fact, some might suggest that PBL represents a direct alternative to today's emphasis on educational standards as measured by high-stakes testing. Some would even argue that the emphasis on static content standards as measured by most such assessments is the very antithesis of the types of deep conceptual understandings that are fostered by PBL (Grant, 2010).

While such a debate might be interesting in the abstract, the research has superseded this question. In spite of early concerns to the contrary, research has clearly proven that PBL, when compared directly with traditional standards-based instruction, does indeed result in higher academic achievement overall as measured on state-wide, standards-based assessments (Boaler, 2002; Geier et al., 2008; Stepien et al., 1992; Strobel & van Barneveld, 2008; Thomas, 2000). In short, if teachers initially fear that moving to PBL instruction results in lower achievement scores on the state-mandated assessments, the research can now put their mind at ease; students achieve at higher levels in PBL instruction than in traditional instruction.

> If teachers initially fear that moving to PBL instruction results in lower achievement scores, the research can now put their mind at ease; students achieve at higher levels in PBL instruction than in traditional instruction.

Of course, in order to realize this benefit, teachers should plan their projects rather carefully in order to specifically address the required educational standards within their state or school district. In order to implement PBL in the context of today's emphasis on Common Core State Standards, teachers should plan projects that clearly address the major standards within their curriculum. In the context of using various projects throughout the year in a given course, teachers might use a curriculum-mapping strategy to map each standard within a course to a particular PBL project within that course. Standards that cannot be matched up with a particular project over the course of the year might be addressed through a modification of one of the PBL projects undertaken that year by adding an artifact that addresses that particular standard.

The Role of Instructional Technology in PBL

As noted previously, many terms have been used to represent project-based learning, such as inquiry-based learning or problem-based learning, and this instructional approach has been emphasized at least since the 1980s (Grant, 2010). However, PBL has certainly received increased emphasis recently, resulting from the advent of an amazing array of instructional technologies that are available today

(Boss & Krauss, 2007; Cognition and Technology Group at Vanderbilt, 1992a, 1992b; Cote, 2007). In particular, various computer-based simulations and games have been developed that provide a vehicle for project-based learning (Salend, 2009). These include programs such as the Adventures of Jasper Woodbury, which provides simulated real-world problems in mathematics and mathematical reasoning (Cognition and Technology Group at Vanderbilt, 1992a, 1992b), the Mission to Mars simulation curriculum (Petrosino, 1995), or the Nature Virtual Serengeti, which allows students to experience an African safari through virtual reality (www.xspeditiononline.com/09 vsserengeti.html).

> PBL has certainly received increased emphasis recently, resulting from the advent of an amazing array of instructional technologies that are available today.

While use of many of these new simulation-based instructional curricula has not become widespread as yet, the use of more commonly available technologies is quite frequent in PBL projects. Of course, teachers are typically very comfortable using spreadsheets, teaching with computerized instructional support programs, or having students search the web for information, but teachers may be less fluent in using the more recently evolved applications such as wikis, blogs, social media, or other modern technology tools for instruction. Still, these applications are playing an increasing role in PBL projects of today (Cote, 2007). In fact, it is difficult to imagine a modern PBL example that did not employ some of these technology-based instructional activities, and in the example provided in Chapter 1, the webquest was clearly an integral artifact of that cedar tree harvesting project.

Moreover, according to most proponents of PBL, these modern instructional technologies represent more than merely ways to provide information to students (Cote, 2007; Partnership for 21st Century Skills, 2009). Rather, these proponents argue that these tools are changing the very fabric of schooling by reformulating the teaching/learning process in a fundamental way (Bender & Waller, 2011; Boss & Krauss, 2007). Rather than passive consumers of knowledge, students in PBL projects are now producers of knowledge as their technology-based artifacts are published via the World Wide Web (Bender & Waller, 2011; Cognition and Technology Group at Vanderbilt, 1992a, 1992b; Ferriter & Garry, 2010; Roth & Bowen, 1995; Wilmarth, 2010).

For example, if students develop a video presentation as one artifact required by the sample project in this chapter, that artifact could easily be uploaded to either YouTube or TeacherTube and, thus, disseminated to the entire world (Bender & Waller, 2011; Ferriter & Garry, 2010). For many students, such worldwide publication options

> Modern instructional technologies are changing the very fabric of schooling by reformulating the teaching/learning process in a fundamental way. Students are now producers of knowledge as their artifacts are published on the World Wide Web.

are quite enticing from a motivational standpoint, and clearly today's teachers will need some degree of fluency with these instructional tools to make that type of publication both possible and meaningful as a learning experience.

Of course, this emphasis on technology, while not an absolute requirement in PBL projects, is certainly a common expectation (Boss & Krauss, 2007). The Partnership for 21st Century Skills strongly supports project-based learning for a variety of reasons (2007, 2009), not the least of which is the increased use of modern instructional technologies in this instructional process. They note that modern instructional technologies make collaborative work on PBL projects possible in ways that would not have been possible as recently as 2000 and that PBL projects build technology skills as well as workplace collaboration skills and teaming skills that are needed in the digital workplace of the next century. Specific examples of various technologies that are particularly applicable for PBL are discussed in more detail in Chapter 4.

Challenges for Teachers in Project-Based Learning

With these advantages noted, moving into project-based learning can be somewhat daunting (Grant, 2010), but the ongoing research seems to suggest that as educators move into 21st-century instruction, PBL will play an increased role in the classroom (Partnership for 21st Century Skills, 2009). However, this move must be undertaken with an eye toward the various challenges that PBL entails. First, teachers must determine the degree to which they are comfortable with this instructional approach, as well as the technology that may be required in PBL. While virtually all teachers have undertaken various projects, some have done this more than others, and in many cases, those projects might have been assigned as individual rather than collaborative inquiry-based projects on authentic questions. Depending on one's comfort level, teachers may wish to move into PBL in the subject area in which they feel most comfortable, rather than challenge themselves by diving into PBL projects in every subject in every class at once.

Further, teachers might search out a teaching partner or mentor teacher and then undertake a move toward increased PBL instruction together. In that fashion, several teachers might undertake the task of researching PBL instruction, using the various sources on the Internet prior to diving into a PBL project. In fact, teachers might undertake a PBL project for their classes to complete together. For example, two fifth-grade teachers in the same school might choose to replace their typical instructional unit on the solar system with a project-based learning experience that they design together. In many cases, two heads are better than one in making certain that meaningful, content-rich learning experiences are provided and that all the required standards are covered. Those teachers may even devise ways for students to work with their colleagues in the other class on the project.

> Teachers may wish to move into PBL in the subject area in which they feel most comfortable, rather than challenge themselves by diving into PBL projects in every subject in every class at once. They may also initiate PBL instruction in conjunction with a partner or mentor teacher.

As noted earlier, teachers must initially determine if they wish to move to full-time PBL or use PBL as an adjunct to their unit-based instruction. If teachers are not entirely comfortable with PBL, they may wish to undertake it as a component of an instructional unit or as a support for several consecutive instructional units rather than as a substitution for all unit instruction. In that fashion, those teachers can perfect the art of PBL instruction and allow time for the intensive planning that will be needed to undertake implementation of PBL for the first time (David, 2008; Grant, 2010).

> Teachers must determine if they wish to move to full-time PBL or use PBL as an adjunct to their unit-based instruction.

Another aspect of a teacher's comfort level in PBL instruction involves the changing role of the teacher in this PBL instruction. Rather than serving as information providers (i.e., in a traditional lecture and discussion–based class), PBL requires teachers to serve as facilitators and instructional coaches, as students move through their project activities. For some teachers, this role change might be quite substantial and challenging. For example, as students engage in a discussion of how to structure a particular artifact to best present their project results to the class, teachers may wish to jump into the discussion and impose their thoughts and suggestions rather than remain aloof and allow the students the time they need to reach a meaningful decision themselves. While teachers are generally quite adept at determining when and how to jump into a student discussion, PBL will require that teachers perfect that skill and use that judgment much more frequently than in the traditional classroom. When teachers attempt this PBL instructional approach, it becomes quite clear that the teacher's role has changed to one of facilitator and instructional coach.

> Rather than serving as information providers, PBL requires teachers to serve as facilitators and instructional coaches, as students move through their project activities.

Next, in initiating a PBL project, teachers must determine the level of choice that students may exercise in identification of the project topic and defining the project parameters. Some advocates of PBL use the phrase "student voice and student choice" to mean that students should exercise nearly complete control of the choices involved in project initiation, from defining the driving question, to identification of the tasks, the artifacts required, and the evaluation criteria to be used (Barrell, 2007; Grant, 2010; Larmer & Mergendoller, 2010). Others suggest that teachers exercise more influence on these determinations (Bender & Crane, 2011; David, 2008), and different teachers provide varying levels of guidance on these questions.

While student voice and choice should be quite apparent throughout the process, since more choice is likely to elicit higher levels of participation, there are advantages to teachers exercising some control over project parameters. When teachers assist in these determinations to a larger degree, there is more assurance that the PBL experience will cover specified objectives and educational standards. Also, even if teachers make these initial determinations on the project content, the driving question, and project requirements, student choice can still be exercised when determining what types of project formats to undertake or how to complete the various requirements. Also, as a given teacher employs PBL instruction, these determinations may vary from one PBL project to another in the class. Even within the same project, teachers may choose to assist one group more than another in making these selections as one way to differentiate the content of the PBL experience.

Finally, teachers should consider their course of action if their first attempt at PBL doesn't work out as well as they hoped. Imagine moving into a science project that is designed as the basis of two entire instructional units that would normally take two weeks each. As the teacher and students move through the planning of the PBL activities and the research experiences, the teacher begins to feel that students, while engaged with the process, are not truly committed to the project as initially hoped. This worry might only be compounded if, at the end of the four-week project, the students don't seem to have mastered the content that was covered. Does this type of result mean that teachers should abandon PBL altogether and scurry back to the more traditional types of unit-based instruction?

While PBL projects generally are successful, as shown by the research results earlier, there are times when a particular project doesn't seem to have the intended effects for a variety of reasons. If the results of a PBL project are not as positive as teachers might hope, there are a number of things teachers can do rather than abandon PBL altogether. These include devising new ways to plan the project with increased student involvement, running project ideas by another teacher more experienced in PBL, floating PBL ideas on one of the blogs associated with this instructional approach, undertaking some professional development in PBL using free Internet resources or readings, or selecting a PBL from the Internet or other curricula source that has proven successful. An excellent discussion of this problem is presented in a blog on PBL instruction (see the website www.edutopia.org/blog/project-based-learning-not-giving-up-suzie-boss). In short, less-than-optimal results in an initial PBL project should not result in wholesale abandonment of this approach but, rather, in a refocusing of effort, and support of a friendly colleague who is likewise engaged in PBL instruction can provide more support than nearly anything else.

Schoolwide PBL Instructional Approaches

As the focus of the discussion earlier indicates, this book is intended to assist individual teachers who wish to undertake PBL instruction within their classroom. In fact, the PBL instructional approach is frequently undertaken by individual teachers, though working with a collaborating teacher to move toward PBL-based instruction is certainly recommended. However, there are numerous examples of entire schools that have chosen to build the whole curriculum around PBL instruction. The website for King Middle School in Portland, Maine, is one example (http://king.portlandschools.org/files/onexpedition/onexpedition.htm). At that website readers can review descriptions of the types of PBL projects undertaken at each grade level and get an understanding of what PBL might look like in such a school. Also, in order to understand the broad movement toward PBL nationally, as well as the ongoing catalysts for that movement, teachers should be aware of the various schools and networks of schools across the United States and around the world that have driven this growing emphasis on PBL.

> There are numerous examples of entire schools that have chosen to build the whole curriculum around PBL instruction.

While such a move toward schoolwide reform is clearly beyond the purview of an individual teacher, some understanding of these PBL-based school networks is advisable, as teachers undertaking PBL projects will come across these entities. This section describes several such PBL efforts that are prominent and provides websites that can be investigated for each.

EdVisions Schools

EdVisions Schools is a network of schools founded and built around exciting, involved project-based learning experiences (www .edvisionsschools.org). In 1993 and 1994, a group of Minnesota educators concerned with the overall quality of schooling got together and reflected on educational options for enhancing the school experience, and that resulted in the creation of the Minnesota New Country School in 1994. That school was founded on the basis of project-based learning principles, as they were first enumerated by John Dewey in 1900 to exemplify his "learning by doing" principles. The school faculty chose to have students plan projects within the curriculum, and they then worked the state-mandated curricular standards into those projects, a process they refer to as backward planning. They believed that this provided a more engaging curriculum than the alternative of beginning with the educational standards and constructing units of instruction around them. They built an interdisciplinary curriculum where projects covered a variety of related subjects, and personalized learning built around commonly available technologies would be one of their guiding principles. Finally, the group decided that teachers should make the major educational decisions on what was best for their students, so they empowered teachers by creating a cooperative that actually owns the school. Thus, the EdVisions Cooperative became a vehicle for teacher ownership of the schools in which they teach.

In 2000, representatives of the Bill and Melinda Gates Foundation visited the school, and their beliefs in the positive vision of the EdVisions school enabled the foundation to offer a series of grants that allowed the school to replicate itself across the nation. Through that funding, a teacher/leader center has been created, and a variety of professional learning experiences are offered ranging from summer institutes on the EdVisions model to actual mentoring of other schools that wish to adopt this model of instruction. Most of these school-to-school mentorships cover a three-year implementation period. Presently more than 40 schools nationwide are operating within the EdVisions school network. Most of these are in Minnesota or Wisconsin, but a number are in Nevada and California, and individual schools are scattered in other states around the country.

Expeditionary Learning Schools

The Expeditionary Learning Schools network (http://elschools .org/our-results/gallery) includes more than 150 schools across the nation that teach all or part of their curriculum via expeditionary learning. This approach involves PBL projects that include actually going to various settings to complete project-based learning experiences and address problems within that specific setting. Of course such expeditions are undertaken only after extensive educational preparation for the expedition and research on the setting and the presenting project or problem. The students then undertake their respective projects and produce high-quality, meaningful work that contributes to the community beyond the classroom. Because projects are carefully mapped to educational standards for each grade level, the students are involved in a skills-rich set of projects that result in products for real-world audiences, which provides an additional reason to strive for excellence. Further, on their website, this organization presents evidence to show that students in these schools outperform students in more traditional instructional approaches on standardized assessments associated with state curricular standards.

Edutopia

Edutopia (edutopia.org) is an online community of educators dedicated to a variety of innovative instructional approaches that include PBL, social-emotional learning, and technology-based learning. The site provides lists of schools with specific emphasis on PBL instruction and sample projects that can be investigated by grade levels. Every teacher who is considering implementation of PBL should investigate this website. In this community, teachers can sign up for a weekly newsletter, join blog discussions on PBL, share their own experiences with PBL, and read about the experiences of others using PBL or any of the other innovative curricular approaches.

Conclusions

This chapter provided insight into how PBL fits into instruction today and discussed using PBL as an adjunct to or a replacement of unit-based instruction. Examples of PBL projects in the literature include both of these approaches. Also, various teaching issues in the PBL context were likewise discussed. PBL does involve a major shift in instructional responsibility in which the teacher ceases to serve as information provider and, rather, serves as facilitator of learning in the context of problem solution. The research presented herein has shown this to be an excellent way to engage students, to increase student motivation and achievement, and to differentiate instruction such that all learners can meaningfully participate.

However, in spite of this research on the efficacy of PBL, a move to PBL instruction can be quite daunting for teachers at first. Still, individual teachers around the nation have initiated exciting projects, and most have experienced PBL quite positively, noting the higher engagement of their students with the learning content. The next chapter presents strategies for designing PBL projects, as well as various additional examples of PBL instruction.

3

Designing
Project-Based
Learning Projects

Planning for PBL Essentials

As noted previously, design of PBL projects can be a challenging task and should never be undertaken lightly. However, with careful attention to the essentials in a PBL project, the design process is manageable. The previous chapters presented definitions of the various essential components of PBL projects, and teachers should begin the design process with these in mind, as illustrated below.

A Project Anchor

An "anchor" of some type is typically used to introduce a project and to generate students' interest in the project. Anchors may be as simple as a one- or two-paragraph narrative that describes a project or problem to consider, as was the case in the cedar tree harvest project presented in Chapter 1. However, the anchor may also be more involved, such as a video segment that presents a problem, a relevant YouTube video that the teacher locates prior to the PBL lesson, or excerpts from a local or national newscast that describe a problem or issue to be considered. Larmer, Ross, and Mergendoller (2009) emphasize the use of correspondence (real or fictitious) that might present the actual anchor. For example, in the cedar tree harvest project, an e-mail from a family member might be presented that describes the disagreement in the family about the possible harvest, desires and concerns of various family members about the view from the plantation home, and specific questions that the family wants answered as a part of the project. Such an e-mail will emphasize the authenticity of the project.

Teachers can be quite creative in developing anchors for PBL projects, and because student buy-in is the ultimate goal of the anchor, every effort should be made to delineate anchors for PBL projects that will help students become interested in the problem to be solved. In fact, the importance of the anchor cannot be overstated; the anchor should provide a compelling reason for students to want to undertake a particular project or problem, and thus, it is important for the anchor to illustrate or describe a real-world project for students to consider. In most cases, the anchor itself may also include either specific information on how the ultimate product(s) might be published or used or at least suggestions for possible use. Again, knowing that a product of a PBL experience has real-world value in that sense is likely to increase students' engagement and motivation to participate.

> Every effort should be made to delineate anchors for PBL projects that will help students become interested in the problem to be solved.

A Driving Question

The driving question is the major focus of the PBL experience. This may be developed by the teacher in advance, or if time allows, student teams may be used to develop this question as a part of the project itself (Barell, 2007; Larmer & Mergendoller, 2010). In conjunction with the anchor, the driving question should both engage students' attention and focus their efforts on the specific information they need to address the problem. PBL projects are long-term, may involve many weeks of work, and cover instructional content over several instructional units. For that reason, it is quite possible, indeed somewhat likely, that students might become "lost" in the possible selections of various content associated with a specific PBL project over time. The purposes of the driving question are to both motivate students and to help students within the project delineate specific parameters that guide their work.

For example, in the cedar tree harvest plantation project in Chapter 1, students would need to understand the growth differences between the two most common types of cedar trees found in the terrain in question, but they would not need to spend time researching growth rates of cedar trees that might be found in high mountain climates above 8,000 or 10,000 feet. In that case, the driving question was, "How many cedar trees in that terrain can be harvested?" and the anchor paragraph stipulated that the plantation was in Virginia, a state that does not have any high mountain terrain even approaching 8,000 feet. In fact, only two types of cedar trees were relevant to the project, and thus, both the anchor and the driving question described the problem and likewise provided a focus to guide students' research on that question.

Of course, teachers realize that virtually every topic imaginable can be researched and investigated at various levels. To address that reality, both the anchor and the driving question together should let students know what information they need to gather, and at what depth, in order to address the problem. In this case, it was clear that students needed only enough information on growth rates to address the question concerning how quickly the harvested cedar trees would be replaced by new cedar trees and that no further information on growth rates would be required.

Finally, the driving question itself should stimulate other, more specific questions. In the early brainstorming sessions during the PBL process, students will be identifying and prioritizing the importance of many specific questions that relate to the driving question. Also, other questions that might arise in open-ended brainstorming sessions might be, after some discussion and reflection, deemed not critically related to the driving question. Thus, those questions would be discarded, and in that sense, a specific, well-stated driving question helps frame the overall PBL task for the student teams.

Student Choice and Student Voice

For some proponents of PBL, student choice may be the single most important component of a PBL project (Grant, 2010; Larmer & Mergendoller, 2010). Student choice is critical for eliciting active student participation in and ownership of the project, and thus, when students choose to undertake a learning experience of this nature, they are much more likely to actively participate in all phases of the learning process if they have considerable choice on which questions to address and which activities to undertake. Further, when students see that they are tackling a real-world problem and seeking a real-world solution for that problem, they become even more motivated. Thus, student choice and student voice is critical for PBL.

Student choice is critical for eliciting active student participation in and ownership of the project.

Of course, when and how to provide students choices are instructional decisions that must be made by the teacher. For example, students might be involved in the actual selection or generation of the driving question on which a project is based, or they might become involved after a driving question has been determined by the teacher. In the latter case, students could still exercise considerable choice in brainstorming how projects are implemented.

In part, this issue of how much choice to provide for students might be initially determined by both students' age and the students' prior experiences in PBL projects. Older students who are used to active participation in PBL experiences might be more equipped to help determine a driving question that would help focus the activities within the project, whereas younger students who have not been exposed to this instructional approach might require a bit more guidance.

Some teachers develop project anchors and driving questions, present those to the students, and then set up student teams to address the problem. In an example described by Larmer and Mergendoller (2010), a teacher introduced an instruction unit on infectious disease in her high school biology class by using a video of a beautiful beach that showed a sign saying "Beach Closed: Contaminated Water." The teacher followed that video with a discussion of when students had seen or read about beaches closed and the types of diseases or pollution that might result in the closing of beaches. Thus, in this case, both the anchor and the driving question were selected by the teacher, and student choice would be involved in planning the research activities to address the problem, researching the question, and developing the artifacts or a presentation on the problem solution.

Other teachers provide merely an anchor that presents a general problem and begin the instruction by having students articulate the driving question. Still other teachers might provide an anchor and then articulate two or three driving questions that become the basis of work for different groups of students. In that instance, letting students choose which question to work on will facilitate higher student engagement.

In all of these examples, students will have choices to make in terms of which activities they might undertake to facilitate the research process for their team. Clearly students should have a voice in various aspects of how the project might be undertaken, since the

students themselves will be determining many organizational aspects in
the problem-solving process, and
teachers should encourage the oppor-

> Teachers should encourage the
> opportunity for students' choices
> through the PBL experience.

tunity for students' choices through the PBL experience.

Given this array of choices, teachers who are beginning their initial move into PBL instruction should consider not only what type of
PBL choices will be most meaningful for the students but also what
is most likely to work for the teachers themselves. Moving into PBL
is not something that can or should be undertaken lightly, and while
PBL does seem to be the differentiated instructional approach of the
future (Barell, 2010; Partnership for 21st Century Skills, 2009), teachers must develop their PBL instructional skills over time. In that
light, teachers who are just beginning PBL instruction might be more
comfortable in selecting both the project anchor and the driving
question, since they may feel more comfortable with more control
over the initial structure of the PBL project. There is certainly nothing
wrong in exercising a bit more control over the projects undertaken
until one has a stronger sense of what PBL is and has amassed some
experience in this instructional paradigm, as long as students are
provided with substantive and meaningful choices in other aspects
of the PBL project.

Specific Processes for Investigation and Research

Teachers use a wide variety of instructional procedures in the
investigation phase or step of the PBL process (Barell, 2007; Baron,
2011; Cote, 2007), and a list of these commonly used procedures is
presented in Box 3.1. While this is certainly not an exhaustive list, it
does illustrate that these instructional procedures are, in most cases,
exactly the same general teaching procedures in use currently. Still, as
this list shows, some of the instructional procedures are a bit more
student driven, whereas the teacher takes a leading role in others during the PBL process.

Of course, teachers realize that students at all levels require some
structure, and the initial description of the PBL project should provide that structure to some degree. For example, the sample PBL
project in Chapter 1 provided not only lists of required activities but
also questions that must be answered, a webquest that students were
to complete, and a rubric for evaluation of the project outcomes. All
of these can be viewed as providing structure for the project overall,
and every PBL experience should stipulate some of these specific

Box 3.1 Instructional Procedures Used in PBL

Scaffolded instruction	Teacher modeling	Peer evaluations
Webquests	Minilessons	Team discussions
Instructional videos	Semantic maps	Journaling
Labs and demonstrations	Guest speakers	Think-alouds
Student modeling	Student-driven minilessons	

guidelines for project completion or artifact generation that will help the student teams frame their activities during the project.

However, many other instructional activities usually arise naturally within the project itself. For example, in undertaking the cedar tree harvest project, some teams might brainstorm various approaches to the question concerning how much of the acreage to leave unharvested in order to maintain the view from the plantation house. Other groups might brainstorm other aspects of the project. Still other groups might quickly divide themselves into working groups and begin Internet research on the questions asked in the project. Finally, other groups might undertake more involved planning by not only creating subgroups of students for specific tasks but also by developing time lines for completion of the tasks assigned to various subgroups.

> Many instructional activities arise naturally within the project itself.

All of these processes might well arise from within the team itself, in the context of the PBL instructional unit, and all of these are worthy goals. The point is that only some of the learning activities and learning processes should be stipulated by the initial assignment, and teachers are likely to see groups of students undertake activities that, while highly related to the project itself, were not even considered by the teacher. Unless time for the project is becoming quite limited, these processes should be both encouraged and facilitated by the teacher as authentic learning experiences that approximate how groups function during problem solving in the real world.

Embedded within the PBL experience, and in particular embedded within the first and second research phases or steps in the instruction, teachers will use many research-proven teaching skills. Certainly teacher modeling of problem-solving processes is very appropriate.

Also, scaffolded assistance should be routinely provided either by the teacher within the collaborative instructional process or in any phase or instructional step within the unit.

In addition to these instructional procedures, and the activities that students must complete, some teachers may wish to use minilessons within the context of PBL to present information in a whole-class manner for the students. A minilesson is a very short, topical lesson in which a teacher or a group of students presents specific direct instruction on information that all the PBL teams might need to complete their project. While not all PBL projects involve minilessons, if teachers wish to present some information in a traditional, teacher-led fashion on a classwide or teamwide basis, there is certainly nothing wrong with that.

> A minilesson is a very short, topical lesson in which a teacher or a group of students presents specific direct instruction on information that all the PBL teams might need to complete their project.

However, certain guidelines must be followed in order to remain true to the overall goals and aims for student engagement inherent in the PBL paradigm. First, minilessons should be undertaken when and if students request them on specific topics. While teachers may encourage PBL student teams to consider the option of allowing the teacher to present some information to the entire team, this should not be forced on the students, as student choice and student voice must be respected throughout the process. Next, minilessons should be rare, perhaps occurring only once or twice in a two-week PBL project. They should be highly focused on one topic and very short, involving no more than a 10- to 15-minute time frame.

In that sense, they should truly be a *mini* lesson on one specific issue or question. Also, every effort should be made to present the minilesson in a fashion that is not similar to the traditional teacher-led lecture or discussion. Creative use of an interactive whiteboard (as described in Chapter 4) is recommended if one is available. Finally, having students conduct some or all of the minilessons is desirable if that can be arranged, since such student presentations are likely to stimulate higher student engagement than in a traditional teacher-led lesson.

Student Inquiry and Innovation

With a strong emphasis on student engagement in problems and projects that students find worthwhile, the teacher's role is predominately facilitative in PBL instruction. Teachers using PBL will, in most cases, not be delivering instruction themselves, and thus, they will have more time for facilitative coaching of teams of students or working with individual students in research or on specific artifact development. In this facilitative role, teachers should use every means at their disposal to stimulate inquiry and reward innovative thought as students move through their planning, research, and artifact development.

> With a strong emphasis on student engagement in problems and projects that students find worthwhile, the teacher's role is predominately facilitative in PBL instruction.

In PBL, the inquiry emphasis begins with the driving question and continues as students, on the first day, reflect on the question, discuss it, and generate additional questions. Also, if teachers choose to include minilessons in their PBL units, those can be structured as highly focused inquiry-based discussions of various issues within a PBL unit. For example, in the tree harvesting unit presented in Chapter 1, teachers might offer students options for minilessons on a variety of topics such as the following:

- What trees grow in wetlands besides cedars? Do these trees impact the cedars or limit growth of the cedars? How does one living thing in a biosphere impact others?
- What impact does clear-cut tree harvesting have on the environment?
- What is the relationship between economics and the protection of specific environments? What other examples can be shown to depict that relationship?

Collaboration and Teamwork

Knowing how to work with a group of individuals to solve a problem is, in many ways, one of the most important skills any young person can develop, since this is a critical workplace skill for virtually every 21st-century job. As students become adept in PBL instructional experiences, they will also become seasoned team players who are used to planning activities as a team, specifying roles for various team members, working together to solve problems, supporting each other's ideas, and offering appropriate and helpful peer evaluations of each other's performance. Instructional procedures such as cooperative instruction, peer tutoring, and reciprocal teaching frequently characterize PBL instruction, and these are discussed in more detail in Chapter 4. In this context, we need only state that helping students learn to work together toward problem solutions is one of the most important outcomes of PBL, and teachers should make every effort to facilitate appropriate collaboration and teamwork.

> Knowing how to work with a group of individuals to solve a problem is one of the most important skills gained in PBL, since this is a critical workplace skill for virtually every 21st-century job.

Opportunities for Reflection

Reflection on one's work is a powerful tool for improvement, and for that reason, creating opportunities for student reflection within the PBL experience is stressed by virtually all proponents of PBL (Barell, 2007; Baron, 2011; Belland et al., 2009; David, 2008; Ghosh, 2010; Laboy-Rush, 2011; Larmer & Mergendoller, 2010; Mergendoller et al., 2007). Reflective thinking prepares students to more actively develop deep-thinking skills and thus attack problems in innovative ways.

> Reflective thinking prepares students to more actively develop deep-thinking skills, and structuring opportunities for reflective thinking is a major emphasis within PBL.

However, as noted, reflective thinking is not an "after the fact" process in PBL, but actually begins with reflections on the project anchor and driving question on the first day of the project. Both group reflection and individual reflection are emphasized, and these types of reflection involve different skills. For example, some teachers using a PBL framework actually teach students the primary guidelines for brainstorming, including the following:

- All ideas are respected as worthy of consideration initially;
- Some may be rejected later as not critical or relevant; but
- During the initial brainstorming exercise, all ideas should be stated and listed for consideration.

In addition to the early project brainstorming by the entire class, reflective brainstorming should also be encouraged at various points after teams are formed. During that phase, the specific questions generated by the whole class could be considered, and various ideas or question topics might be adopted by the group. Also, during this second phase of brainstorming, some of the original ideas might be rejected by the group as redundant with other suggestions or as unnecessary for project completion. Teachers will serve a facilitating role in this process and can help students develop their brainstorming, idea consideration skills.

Finally, in addition to whole-class, or team-based reflection sessions, individual reflection on the content and the overall PBL

Individual reflection via journaling on the content and the overall PBL experience is strongly encouraged in PBL instruction.

experience is strongly encouraged in PBL instruction (Baron, 2011; Laboy-Rush, 2011; Larmer & Mergendoller, 2010). To facilitate such reflection on an individual level, students are frequently encouraged to journal during the PBL project (Barell, 2007).

Journaling involves writing about the big ideas that emerge from the PBL research or artifact development and thus offers opportunity for deep reflections on the meaning of the educational content. Also, journaling provides an opportunity for highly differentiated instruction, since some students will require more support for their journaling activities than others.

For example, highly articulate students with few reading or writing difficulties may merely be assigned to "keep a journal about completing this PBL project and make a paragraph-long entry at least every other day." In that case, the teacher should periodically read sections from each student's journal and discuss those ideas with the students during the PBL process.

In contrast, other students are likely to require more support for their journaling activity. Some students might be provided sentence starters for their journals that help them prepare their entries, or get them going, and those sentence starters may be varied by where the student is within the PBL experience. A set of such sentence starters that may be used at different phases within a PBL unit is presented in Box 3.2.

Feedback and Revision

Feedback is a critical component of PBL instruction, and because the teacher is serving as facilitator, he or she is likely to have more time for individual and team feedback than in a traditional instructional class. Feedback can be based on teacher evaluation, self-evaluation, or peer evaluations. As students mature, the importance of using both self-evaluations and peer evaluations increases, since those skills are likely to be desired in the vocational future of many students, and PBL instruction provides many opportunities for such evaluation.

Evaluative feedback can be either formative (i.e., evaluation taking place during the PBL process to help students form or refocus their work as necessary) or summative (final evaluation taking place at the end of the project). In the PBL learning environment both types of feedback are provided, but formative evaluation opportunities

---

Box 3.2 Sentence Starters for a Journal Entry in a PBL Project

Initial journal sentence starters (used for first two or three days in the unit)

Based on our first discussion, we need to find out . . .

I can contribute to my team by . . .

I don't understand . . .

I know I need to look up several things including . . .

Journal sentence starters for the research phase (used from Day 2 or 3 until the final days of the unit)

In my research I have discovered that . . .

I found it amazing that . . .

It was awesome when we discovered that . . .

What if . . .

I wonder if this idea _____ connects with this one _____?

Journal sentence starters for later in the PBL unit (used in the second research phase and through the end of the unit)

It was amazing that . . .

I was really surprised when . . .

This idea _____ relates to my studies in _____ because _____.

---

abound. In fact, much more emphasis is typically placed on formative evaluation and feedback in the PBL process simply because teachers are doing such formative evaluations virtually all the time. Such formative evaluation may involve a discussion of team progress or merely an informal comment on a student's artifact or research progress.

> Evaluative feedback can be either formative or summative, and in the PBL learning environment both types of feedback are provided, but formative evaluation opportunities abound.

Certainly each time a team meeting is held, the teacher should sit in and offer verbal feedback on what planning the team has accomplished, what is completed, and what is yet to be done. Also, teachers should keep a close eye on the development of the prototype artifacts as individual students or small groups of students begin to develop those

> Each time a team meeting is held, the teacher should sit in and offer verbal feedback on what the team has accomplished, what is completed, and what is yet to be done.

artifacts. Comments can then be offered on additional information that might be included within the artifact, and such informal evaluation is the hallmark characteristic of the facilitative role of the teacher in the PBL experience.

Further, PBL projects provide a number of additional assessment options including self-evaluations and peer evaluations. Teachers can be highly creative as they develop a variety of ways for students to do self- or peer evaluations, most of which will be focused to provide formative feedback in support of students on their PBL team. These evaluation and assessment options are discussed in more detail in Chapter 6.

Next, summative evaluation and feedback from outside the classroom are encouraged, such that once a team's artifacts or project presentation is published, every effort should be made to gather evaluation data from the target audience if at all possible. An example of this might be the publication of an artifact or report in a local newspaper or a link from that newspaper's website to the school website where a video podcast from the project can be displayed. In each published article or podcast, an invitation could be extended requesting that the general public communicate their responses to the school on the PBL project. While this is not always possible, such feedback does emphasize the authentic nature of the class activities, and the students will begin to feel that their work makes a real difference. Of course, regardless of the possibility of receiving outside independent feedback, each teacher will provide summative evaluations for each project in the process of assigning grades to the students. Those assessment and grading options in PBL are discussed in more detail in Chapter 6.

Finally, at each phase of artifact development evaluative feedback will be provided in some form, and the various artifacts will be revised or redeveloped to address any problems identified in the feedback (Barell, 2007). The opportunity to redo or revise an artifact is important, and even students who may have been reluctant to complete such work in the past will undertake meaningful revisions in PBL since they know their work has authentic meaning and will be

> Even students who may not have completed work in the past will undertake meaningful revisions in PBL classes since they know their work has authentic meaning and will be published in some form.

published in some form for the class, the school, or the larger community. In short, virtually all students want to put their best work forward in the PBL instructional environment, and this will motivate them to actively participate in revisions of their work.

Public Presentation of the Project Results

PBL projects are intended to be authentic examples of the types of problems students confront in the real world, so some public presentation or publication of project results is a critical emphasis within PBL (David, 2008; Ghosh, 2010; Grant, 2010; Larmer & Mergendoller, 2010). Students will value what they see their teachers value, and presentation of the class's work to others in the community is one way to show the value of that work. This is, perhaps, the main reason that student engagement tends to be so much higher in PBL learning experiences.

Of course, publication opportunities are limited only by the teacher's and the classes' collective imaginations. Publication can involve a variety of outlets for the culminating project or any artifacts that the class chooses to publish. For example, video artifacts can be uploaded to YouTube at the discretion of the teacher and the class. Alternatively, short videos showing students' work may be uploaded to school websites. Written reports can be structured as short articles for local newspapers or perhaps as letters to the editor or government representatives. Presentations for groups outside of the school can be held.

> Publication opportunities are limited only by the imagination and involve a variety of outlets for the culminating project from YouTube to school websites.

When considering publication outlets, teachers are well advised to consider the students' level of exposure. For example, worldwide publication options include uploading a video prepared by the class to YouTube, or other Internet venues, whereas a more limited publication might involve placing the same video on the website for the school. While school websites are certainly available worldwide via the Internet, they are not as likely to be found in routine searches as perhaps YouTube videos might be. Also, prior to using an outlet such as YouTube for publication of student work, teachers should consult with their principal to see if any school district regulations apply. Of course, the safety of students is a critical concern, and in no instance should student names, personal information, or addresses be provided in the published work.

With that said, many publication options are available, and some of these are listed in Box 3.3. In one PBL experience a middle school class conducted a study of the value of the wetlands behind the school to help the local school board determine the advisability of using that land for a school extension. That PBL project resulted in a video that presented legal, engineering, and financial issues in using that land in that fashion. This was shown at a school board

---

Box 3.3 Publication Options for PBL Artifacts

Local newspapers   Local television outlets
Student presentations at   School websites
PTA/PTO evenings   School media centers
Local libraries   Local magazines
Local governance meetings   Class blogs
Presentations at local clubs   Class blogs
(e.g., Lions)   Topical magazines
Letters to the editor
Letters to house
representatives/senators

---

meeting and then placed as a DVD in the community public library. Again, publication options are nearly endless, but a few are presented here.

Preplanning Questions for Designing a PBL Experience

With these characteristics or essential components of PBL instruction in mind, teachers can consider planning their first PBL instructional unit. The first step in moving into PBL is the preplanning phase that must be undertaken by teachers. In this text the term *preplanning* is used for teachers' planning, whereas the term *planning* is used to refer to the students' planning of the PBL activities once the project has begun.

There are a number of preplanning questions and issues that should be addressed prior to beginning the PBL unit, as these preplanning activities lead to the construction of a meaningful PBL experience for the students. Consideration of these preunit planning questions and activities, presented in Box 3.4, should help assure a valid and content-rich instructional learning experience.

> Preplanning questions and activities must be undertaken by the teacher prior to beginning the PBL project to assure a valid and content-rich instructional learning experience.

Common Core State Standards and State Standards

As noted in Chapter 2, many states have adopted the Common Core State Standards (www.corestandards.org/the-standards) as the basis for instruction, and PBL instruction can be founded on these

---

| **Box 3.4 Preplanning Teacher Activities and Issues** |

1. What standards can be covered?

2. What technology resources are available?

3. How long will preparation of instructional resources take?

4. What other resources are available for the planned project?

5. What is the planning time frame for a PBL unit?

Common Core State Standards as well as other standards in states such as Texas that have chosen not to adopt these standards (again, for information on how PBL fits with state standards other than the Common Core, please see the appendix).

Once a teacher determines how to work a PBL learning experience into his or her curricular schedule for a given academic year, the next issue involves which of the Common Core State Standards should be and can be tied to the PBL experience. The Common Core State Standards, of course, are standardized across states, but previously developed content standards differ from state to state. In many state standards, the curricular guides are delineated in terms of broad content standards that represent the big ideas that students should master from the curriculum and smaller "indicators," "benchmarks," or "substandards" that are related to each standard. Thus, accompanying each standard, most state curricula include substandards, sometimes called benchmarks, that present the specific items that might be used to show students have mastered a given standard.

These benchmarks are typically much more numerous than the standards themselves but represent merely indicators of content mastery and not mandated items to cover in the curriculum, at least in most states. Thus, in most states, the expectation is that all students cover content associated with all educational standards, in order to master those standards, but that they should not necessarily cover content related to all of the substandards.

Therefore, when teachers are considering which standards to cover within a PBL instructional project (or for that matter, any instructional unit), those teachers should target all of the curricular standards, and as many substandards as possible, and tie those to specific required assignments, artifacts, or products within the PBL unit. When teachers are using the Common Core State Standards, this is fairly easy, since again, those are clear, specific, and generally represent the big ideas or important tasks within the curriculum. Thus, the Common Core State Standards represent an opportunity for education to shift away from more narrow, test prep–types of instruction to focus on deeper understanding of the big ideas and problem-solving opportunities within the curriculum.

Thus, in preparing for PBL, teachers are wise to focus on the Common Core State Standards or the educational standards in their state. As a teacher contemplates the types of required products or artifacts to place in a PBL unit, that teacher might tie two or three of the Common Core State Standards to that product or learning experience, and with multiple assigned tasks within the PBL project, teachers most often find that they can cover the required Common Core State Standards, or any other set of educational standards, for a given time frame fairly easily.

> Teachers should target all of the curricular standards, and as many substandards as possible, and tie those to specific required assignments, artifacts, or products within the PBL unit.

It is important to note two things relative to content coverage of curricular standards in PBL instructional paradigms. First, research has consistently shown that PBL results in higher levels of mastery of curricular standards than does traditional instruction (Barell, 2007; Belland et al., 2009; Geier et al., 2008; Gijbels et al., 2005; Grant, 2010; Mergendoller et al., 2007; Strobel & van Barneveld, 2008). Of course, the research cited here involved state standards, rather than the more recently developed Common Core State Standards, but there is every reason to believe that students will succeed more on assessments related to the Common Core State Standards in PBL instruction than in traditional instruction.

Second, like many other differentiated instructional approaches, students working on a PBL project are more inclined to learn content from working together, and thus, many of the substandards or curricular benchmarks within state standards will be addressed in the process of completing the various assignments and products within the PBL learning experience, without the teacher having to lead a classwide discussion on every particular item in the curriculum. Of course, technology can make this process of mapping content standards onto PBL projects somewhat easier, and teachers should explore resources for that task at the state department of education website. A simple Internet search on curriculum mapping tools can also assist teachers in finding such tools for mapping content standards to PBL projects.

Nevertheless, the importance of this preplanning activity cannot be overstated. Teachers must specifically identify the content standards associated with the PBL instructional unit to assure coverage of the required content. Further, in this process, teachers may be freed from previous curricular time frame expectations. It is often the case that, while planning a PBL unit, teachers find that content that might typically be covered much later in the year can easily be placed within an earlier PBL unit. In that case, teachers should feel free to place those curricular standards in the earlier PBL unit. Thus, the lockstep nature of the traditional standards-based curriculum becomes somewhat more flexible in PBL units.

Finally, teachers may choose to emphasize standards more directly by identification of specific standards in the PBL project itself. For example, in designing specific projects for a yearlong curriculum in a particular grade level, once the teacher has "mapped out" where the required standards fit in various projects, the standards themselves might be listed on the project descriptions that are provided to the students (Boss & Krauss, 2007; Schlemmer & Schlemmer, 2008). Teachers might choose to add a section under the project anchor that includes curricular standards addressed by that project and thereby emphasize for the students the importance of the project within the context of their individual classes.

What Technology Resources Are Available?

Because technology plays such a significant role in PBL instruction, knowing what technology resources are available can be critical, and PBL in the 21st century is increasingly technology based (Boss & Krauss, 2007). Further, given the focus in this text on individual teachers undertaking PBL instruction, the technology resources question becomes increasingly important.

Ideally, every student would have a computer on his or her desk with immediate Internet access for research, as well as writing and presentation software (Baron, 2011). However, this is rarely the reality in schools today, and even in situations where computers and Internet access is quite limited, PBL may still be initiated. For example, nearly every school has computer labs that can be used on specific days within a PBL experience in which students could find Internet access. Also, small groups of students can typically be allowed to go to the media center to undertake specific research for a brief time during a given class period.

Still, use of 21st-century technologies is a major emphasis within the growing movement toward PBL instruction (Baron, 2011; Boss & Krauss, 2007; Cote, 2007; Partnership for 21st Century Skills, 2009), and thus, every effort should be made to build PBL on innovative use of modern technologies. Again, this is seen by many proponents as one hallmark of PBL overall (Baron, 2011; Cote, 2007; Partnership for 21st Century Skills, 2009; Salend, 2009).

How Long Will Preparation of Instructional Resources Take?

Proponents of PBL generally agree that PBL instruction is front-loaded in terms of the time required for project planning and design (Boss & Krauss, 2007; Larmer et al., 2009). Beyond merely access to the Internet, the teacher must prepare instructional assignments, review informational websites, develop various webquests for those websites, seek videos that might be helpful, plan options for portfolio development by student teams, develop anchors for each planned project, as well as a driving question that together will motivate the students, and develop rubrics to guide various project assignments or project artifacts. If students are expected to develop videos, gather photographs, or use presentation software for the project, equipment and other resources for those activities must be obtained. As this list of resource preparation activities indicates, PBL experiences do not just "happen"!

In most modern PBL experiences one or more webquests are required assignments in the research phase of the project, and these must be developed in advance by the teacher. Of course, if a teacher implements a PBL experience he or she finds on the Internet, much of this resource preplanning work can be accomplished by seeing what others have developed and adapting those activities. Still, teachers should not move into a PBL unit without having done all of these preparatory resource development steps, any more than they would initiate any other instructional unit without having the unit thoroughly planned in advance.

In most PBL assignments, teachers include lists of resources that students must at least review and consider for their project. Such lists will grow over time, as the PBL instructional project is used from year to year, since both teachers and students will find additional resources or websites relevant to the project. For some websites or topics, a webquest or specific artifact might be assigned, while other resources might be listed as potentially helpful but not required of every student or PBL team. Again, finding these resources in advance of the PBL instructional unit will take some teacher time.

With that time consideration noted, there are several bits of good news here. First, much of this type of resource development is required for any instructional unit, so while PBL might add some time requirements in this process, teachers do much of this work anyway. Second, once a PBL unit is planned, it can be replicated the next year, or in other class periods during the same year, with relative ease. Next, as teachers review websites or videos for one project, they often find resources that apply to other PBL projects later in the year. Therefore, by taking careful note of these resources, they will be better prepared for preparation of subsequent PBL projects. Finally, it is almost always the case that students find additional resources for a given topic, and teachers should certainly incorporate those resources into the project for future years. Thus, those additions will save considerable teacher time. In effect, the project design process, while taking some time, may be viewed as paying off not only in the next PBL project, but in subsequent projects or even in next year's work as well.

> Once a PBL unit is planned, it can be replicated the next year, or in other class periods during the same year, with relative ease.

What Other Resources Are Available for the Planned Project?

In addition to technology resources, various projects may be facilitated with other types of resources. For example, if a high school social studies class is undertaking a study of the Vietnam War (1965–1973), access to veterans who fought during that war would be of great benefit. The teacher's contacts within that community, or the contacts of other teachers, could be used to access those veterans for individual student interviews. In that sense, consideration of resource availability is critical in planning rich PBL experiences.

Further, preplanning consideration of resources for research can help determine what projects not to undertake. One school near the seacoast in Maine was undertaking a project on how sunken boats impact marine life. However, as they considered the available resources, the faculty discovered that there were not enough sunken ships and boats in safe locations for students to study, and as a result, they refocused their project topic (Baron, 2011).

Finally, some PBL instruction involves actual field trips, or expeditions, to locations under study, as discussed in Chapter 2. If the PBL experience is intended to involve an actual expedition, the teacher will have to preplan that expedition to the setting involved in the PBL project. Arranging such field trips can take considerable time, since parental permissions must be obtained for such student travel, and all activities to be completed at the setting have to be arranged in advance. Again, most PBL projects do not involve actual expeditionary experiences, but some do, and while costly in terms of preparation and planning time, these can be very rewarding learning experiences overall.

What Is a Realistic Planning Time Frame for PBL?

With these time concerns noted, teachers might well ask, What is the time frame for preplanning a PBL unit? Virtually all proponents of PBL state that PBL instruction is somewhat involved and will take somewhat more time than planning traditional instructional units (Barell, 2007; Gijbels et al., 2005; Grant, 2010; Mergendoller et al., 2007; Strobel & van Barneveld, 2008). However, virtually every one of these proponents likewise assures teachers that moving toward PBL instruction is worth that extra time, with the payoff coming in terms of student motivation and ultimate mastery not only of curricular content but also of technology and team-working skills needed in the 21st century.

The planning time frame will vary from one teacher to the next and one project to the next, depending on the level of planning the teacher chooses to undertake. Also, as teachers become more fluent in preparation of this type of lesson, they develop skills for developing webquests, identifying Internet resources, and developing liaisons in the community to assist with publication options. As teachers hone and refine those skills, the planning time will decrease a bit, and again, the payoff in terms of student interest, engagement, and increased academic scores is well worth the effort.

With these variables in mind, it is quite difficult to provide a specific answer to the question of how much planning time PBL will take. However, as a general recommendation, teachers should do planning over a period of three to four weeks at a minimum, by spending some time (perhaps 15 to 25 minutes daily) on exploration of websites, etc. prior to moving into their first PBL unit. By reflecting on the planned PBL experience over that length of time, rather than attempting to plan a PBL unit in six hours over one day, teachers will come up with more ideas than in a more compressed time frame.

Instructional Steps or Phases in the PBL Experience

As this discussion shows, there are considerable differences in how teachers plan and undertake PBL instruction. When the faculty in the entire school chooses to undertake PBL, teachers receive the advantages of collaborative support from their colleagues and the administration, and such support will assist in the preplanning activities delineated earlier. In those conditions, a wide variety of implementation options are likely to arise, as different teachers in the school undertake PBL in various ways and share those options with each other.

However, because this book is intended for teachers moving into PBL instruction individually, and perhaps without the support of all of their colleagues at the school, the more specific the process can be, the more teachers are likely to feel comfortable in initiating PBL within their own classroom. The steps described shortly can provide structure for a teacher's initial foray into teaching via PBL projects, including projects that range in length from two to ten weeks or more. Thus, teachers new to the PBL experience may pick a two-week instructional unit on a topic they are comfortable with and undertake a PBL unit using these steps as both instructional and time frame guidelines. The steps are presented in Box 3.5.

> The more articulate the steps in the instructional process are, the more teachers are likely to feel comfortable in initiating PBL.

Box 3.5 Steps in a PBL Instructional Project

I. Introduction and Team Planning the PBL Project

Review anchor and reflection on driving question

Classwide brainstorming on specific research questions

Assign teams for the PBL experience

Set goals and develop time lines

Division of labor on research questions (everybody has a role)

Assignment of required artifacts and products

II. Initial Research Phase: Gathering Information

Webquests completed herein

Interviews with locals

Review/identify other sources (e.g., YouTube, newspapers, books, media center, etc.)

Minilessons on specific topics might be offered

Evaluation of information form (see Box 4.5, Evaluation of Information From the Internet)

III. Creation, Development, Initial Evaluation of Presentation, and Prototype Artifacts

Storyboard development

Begin downloading videos, images

(Continued)

Box 3.5 (Continued)

Develop prototype (initial) presentation and artifacts

Group evaluation of the prototypes

Formative evaluation of prototype artifacts

IV. Second Research Phase

Seek additional information to develop prototypes more fully

Minilessons on specific topics might be offered

Revision of prototypes and storyboard with new information

V. Final Presentation Development

Storyboard revision/additions

Some write, some speak, some videotape, some edit, some do art, etc.

VI. Publication of Product or Artifacts

Final classwide evaluation (perhaps peer evaluation)

Publication of project or artifacts

Initiation and Team Planning

On the first day of a PBL unit, several whole-class activities are usually undertaken, and these may take from 30 minutes to a whole class period. As noted, prior to beginning the instruction, a teacher will have developed (or selected) some type of anchor to present the project overall and encourage student interest. Videos work wonderfully for that, but paragraph narratives can work as well. Teachers may wish to develop these around a local issue in the news and thus benefit from students who might have more interest in actual happenings near the school. The anchor will then be presented to the whole class on the first day of the PBL project.

Next, the driving question may be developed in advance by the teacher or developed by the students after the anchor is presented (Larmer & Mergendoller, 2010). An effective driving question summarizes the problem or issue, uses compelling language to motivate students, and points to supplementary or secondary questions that need to be addressed. Students should reflect on and discuss the driving question for 10 to 15 minutes as a whole-class activity.

This frequently becomes a lively initial discussion, and often many good ideas emerge in these initial discussions. For that reason, during the discussion activity, the teacher should appoint one student to go to the dry erase board or interactive whiteboard and make note of any additional questions that arise. Those questions can then be shared with PBL teams as their work moves forward.

Then the class should be divided into teams, with the expectation that those teams will work together to solve the problem presented in the PBL experience. Teachers may allow for some student choice in team formation or merely place students into their teams for the project. Generally groups of seven to twelve students can work together effectively as a PBL team, and given the size of a given class, teachers might wish to use either two or three teams for a PBL project. From that point on, each team will be acting relatively independently for the remainder of the PBL unit.

Now some team planning will be necessary. This may involve the last half of the first period in the PBL unit, or it may take the second day of that unit. During this team planning several things must be accomplished and written down by team members. First, teams should be encouraged to set specific goals, given the time frame delineated by the teacher for the project. These may be general goals, or specific timelines, and may vary from team to team. However, the teacher should set the overall parameters (i.e., "We plan to spend 10 days on this project") for the teams to follow in setting up project timelines.

Once teams are formed, a bit more brainstorming may be necessary to generate specific questions the students feel should be addressed, as well as who should research each question. Sometimes, teams develop a "team governance" structure, involving a team leader, a video director, a presenter, and other specific roles for various students on the team, and let that governance structure identify specific tasks for team members, under the guidance of the teacher. This organizational idea, or some type of organizational structure, should be encouraged, and at a minimum, specific role assignments for each student should be articulated during this phase.

> Specific role assignments for each student should be articulated in PBL projects.

Other student roles may include having a student with some talent using digital cameras designated as the "videographer" for the group. Someone with good Internet search skills might be the "lead researcher," while a good writer might be designated as the "storyboard coordinator." Further, these persons may select someone to assist them in their tasks during the project, but everyone on the team should be assigned a role to help all students understand who does what for the team.

In PBL instruction, some assignments are given to each student in the class to complete (this is typically the case with webquests), but other project assignments are not individual. For the team assignments, an "artifact head" or "product coordinator" should be assigned who will have ultimate responsibility for that single product or artifact.

Finally, after making student role assignments within the team, the team should write up a brief summary of their planning and those role assignments. Thus, this step is considered completed when the teacher is presented with a written summary of the team planning. Each team must present to the teacher some written outline of who is assigned various roles and tasks. This can be fairly easily facilitated in the initial team meeting by having one student write down the various specific questions generated, the individual students' roles, and any other product assignments.

As this list of tasks shows, student planning of the PBL activities may take more than one instructional period. However, in most PBL projects, no more than two instructional periods should be allowed for these tasks, and in a two-week instructional unit, much of this introductory and planning work should be completed in one or one-and-a-half instructional periods.

Initial Research Phase: Gathering Information

In well-planned projects, the initial research phase presents fewer unanticipated problems than might arise in later phases of the PBL experience, since the activities within the initial research phase are more likely to be somewhat predictable. Thus, teachers will have already arranged for ample research resources for the project. Internet access is key at this phase, as few projects are undertaken today that do not involve significant time researching various topics on the Internet. For each PBL project one or two webquests will probably be required to assist students in their research, and in most cases, such webquests are required from every student, with the expectation that those be completed in this initial research phase.

In contrast to such predetermined assignments, students will be broadly searching for relevant information that addresses the driving question or the more specific questions that arise in the early brainstorming discussions. Thus, teams will probably pull in photos, short videos, or written reports that may be found online in their research.

For groups of students that are not used to PBL instruction, it may be beneficial to have them complete this initial research phase working in pairs. Not only will that tend to keep them focused on the task at hand, but they may also be more comfortable working with a partner.

If PBL is undertaken in situations where Internet resources are limited, this phase provides an opportunity for the teacher and the teams to consider some creative scheduling to facilitate students' work. Rather than have 25 class members all try to access computers simultaneously, the teacher may randomly select one team to begin their webquests at this point. Thus, in a class of 25 students, only 12 would need computer and Internet access. Further, by having students work in pairs, only six Internet-capable computers might be needed. In many schools smartphones are now used to help provide Internet search access for students, and this might be an option for students who have smartphones available.

The other team, meanwhile, might be assigned to undertake non-Internet based research. Such research could involve traditional library or media center searches, using texts to identify and refine the questions for the PBL experience, taking photos or developing websites for the PBL project, developing interview questions for any guests that might be interviewed for the project, or holding discussions of what the team expects from each team member.

Also, it is during this phase that some teachers present minilessons. In some cases, these are directly related to the assigned tasks within the project, and all class members participate. However, minilessons provided in the context of PBL projects provide an excellent way to differentiate the work. For example, teachers might offer minilessons for smaller groups of students that have the same role responsibility in different teams or for students who might need help with particular concepts within the broader content of the PBL project.

Creation, Development, and Initial Evaluation of Presentation and Prototype Artifacts

This creation phase is likely to overlap to some degree with the initial research phase as well as later phases or steps in the PBL process. While listing steps or phases in sequenced order in this text is intended to help teachers understand the PBL process, teachers should be aware that these steps are merely broad guidelines. For example, the creation of artifacts can begin as soon as students begin their initial research. In the cedar tree harvest project described in Chapter 1, if a student finds a chart of factual information on projected growth of cedars in swamplands on the first day of the research phase, that student should immediately forward a copy of that chart (with appropriate citations) to the product coordinator for the final video presentation. Thus, from the first day of the initial research phase, the creation of artifacts often begins. In fact, there is often considerable overlap between the research phases and the creation of artifacts.

For that reason, the product coordinator for the presentation video and the storyboard writer might have to work together during the initial research phase, incorporating various items into the video presentation as other students locate and forward relevant information. Thus, these students may do somewhat less actual research on the Internet, and more synthesis of the information, as they, working together, develop a storyboard for the final project video presentation.

In contrast, other students on that team might be developing artifacts that are independent of the video presentation. For example, charted data or spreadsheets on projected cedar tree harvests might be one artifact that is developed independently, and students should begin work on a prototype of that chart as soon as the data become available in the initial research phase. Meanwhile, the teacher will be moving from student to student within the class, helping, coaching, suggesting additional resources, and generally facilitating the students' learning.

Toward the end of the creation phase, teams should hold a meeting and review their progress on each required artifact and the final presentation. The overall purpose of that meeting is to determine what required assignments have been completed, what work addressing the driving question has been accomplished, and what additional information should be gathered and incorporated into the project. In PBL projects, students will always be seeking to add to the content and thus enhance the project overall.

For some students, teachers may provide guiding questions to assist in this formative evaluation process. Students might be encouraged to consider their prototype artifacts and the storyboard and ask, "Have we answered the basic questions?" That answer will, in most cases, lead to additional information that should be gathered and incorporated into the project in some fashion.

> Toward the end of the creation phase, teams should hold a meeting and review their progress on each required artifact and the final presentation.

The Second Research Phase

In this phase, students will seek out the information they need to fill the gaps in the overall presentation. Because different teams might pursue different approaches for solving the overall problem, by this phase, it is quite likely that various teams will be seeking different information. Thus, the content and information resources that might be needed in the later stages in the PBL process are somewhat more difficult to predict than in the earlier stages, and teams will vary on what is needed to complete their projects. In some cases, a considerable amount of information might be needed. However, in most instances, because teachers will have been coaching students on the overall quality of the content prior to this phase, only a few additional pieces of information should be required. Of course, major changes in overall PBL project direction should be avoided because as teams approach this phase of their work, the time allocated to the project is probably becoming quite limited.

Finally, any students who have not completed the required individual assignments should complete that work during this phase of the PBL project. In most cases, PBL projects do involve work that is specifically required from all students, and those requirements must be done prior to the final development phase and publication phase.

Final Presentation Development

Any revision of the storyboard, the video segments that have been prepared, or artifacts that result from the second research phase should be undertaken at this step. Because time is probably becoming very limited by this point, only those changes that will significantly enhance the project should be undertaken. Also during this phase, the team should meet as a group and evaluate every artifact and product, either using a structured peer review evaluation format or some other evaluation approach. Peer evaluation as an assessment tool is discussed more extensively in Chapter 6. However, at this point, the peer evaluation should involve only team members and not be a summative peer review done by all members of the class (a classwide peer review will be conducted in the final step of the PBL process). Thus, the goal for this team-based peer review evaluation is to approximate the classwide peer evaluation that is to come in the upcoming publication phase of the project.

Publication of Product or Artifacts

Publication options for PBL projects are nearly unlimited and have been discussed previously. However, teachers must realize that publication of students' work is a critical component of the PBL experience, and students value this aspect of PBL more so than any other.

If students believe they are solving real-world problems that others in the community care about, they are simply going to work harder.

With that noted, the timing of the publication experience may be problematic in certain cases. For example, imagine a high school science class undertaking a PBL project that addresses the driving question, "Should the school board build a parking lot in the lower land behind the current school building or develop a 'wetlands study habitat' with that land?" Of course, this would probably be a long-term interdisciplinary project that might involve teachers in earth sciences, economics, biology, and local politics. In such a project, the "publication" option might be a 30-minute report to the county commission and school board on the advisability of a parking lot versus a study habitat. The report would probably catalogue both the economics of those choices and projected use of both options. However, the review meeting might be scheduled several weeks after the students completed the PBL project, and thus those students would have moved on into other projects or other instructional units; hence the timing problem.

With that problem noted, it is still vital that students do present their PBL project findings on the parking lot versus study habitat question to the county commission and school board. In that situation, the women and men sitting on those elected bodies would probably show considerable interest in what the students had done to reach their recommendations, and that interest from the community is the essential payoff for the students, the sense that their work, their thoughts, and their ideas matter in solving real-world problems. Thus, in spite of timing problems that may arise, every effort should be made to provide students with opportunities to showcase their work for others.

Summary of Six Instructional Phases

These instructional phases or steps have been presented and described to illustrate how a relatively simple two-week PBL project might progress. Of course, these general instructional steps should not be considered "ironclad" examples of all PBL projects. In many longer-term projects, for example, there would probably be several additional research phases and multiple peer evaluations. As in virtually every form of teaching, flexibility is key to PBL instruction. Teachers can never tell when snow days or unscheduled school assemblies will interrupt instruction, and such events will change the instructional schedule for all instruction in the school. Veteran teachers have learned to simply roll with the punches in teaching.

Still, these instructional phases do represent the types of activities that students and teachers will be engaged in during PBL instruction, and using these basic instructional steps as a guide, teachers can readily see how their instructional role is likely to change in PBL instruction. Aside from the one or two minilessons noted in the steps earlier, teachers' instructional efforts will be refocused to facilitate learning experiences rather than deliver initial instruction on new concepts. In short, this is teaching for the 21st century.

A Schedule for a PBL Project

In order to actually show what a PBL project might look like, schedule-wise, we might imagine the cedar tree harvest project that was presented in Chapter 1 as a two-week project for a middle school science class. Box 3.6 presents a schedule of activities that could be used in a unit of instruction that would allow for completing that project in a two-week time frame.

Box 3.6 Schedule for a PBL Project on Cedar Tree Harvest

- Monday: Anchor day and team assignments
- Tuesday: Complete team meetings and begin initial research phase
- Wednesday: Minilesson on swamp ecosystems and continue initial research phase
- Thursday: Continue initial research phase and begin creation phase
- Friday: Complete initial research phase and continue creation phase
- Monday: Complete some artifacts and video segments
- Tuesday: Minilesson on impact of tree harvests on wildlife, complete initial creation, and begin second research phase
- Wednesday: Begin final additions phase
- Thursday: Final team peer evaluation meetings
- Friday: Final presentation and publication phase

On Monday, the first day of the unit, the teacher would present the anchor video on the cedar tree harvest project and conduct a 15-minute discussion of the proposed tree harvest. In that discussion, additional questions students want answered will be noted, and the teacher could then appoint teams. In a project such as this, it might be interesting to appoint students with similar views about a tree harvest to the same team. For example, some students may be generally against tree harvests in any form, and lively discussions can ensue from placing a number of those students together on a team and having them plan a "debate" with the pro–tree harvest team.

Then the teams should review the assignment together and discuss roles for everyone on the team, thus developing their initial plan for the project. Teachers will, as their time allows, sit in on every team meeting, except where two or more teams are having their meetings simultaneously. It is important to provide guidance to the teams, at least initially, and help keep them on track.

On Tuesday, teams will probably need to meet and complete their planning, assuring that all students have a role. In some cases, another brief brainstorming session might be desirable, but by the end of this second day, a written plan should emerge from each team. The team should then present that along with each student's assigned role, to the teacher. At that point, each team member will know his or her task, and several students should begin their initial research on their assigned question. Others may begin completing the required individual assignments such as the webquest.

On Wednesday, teams will continue the initial research phase, and all members should endeavor to complete all individually required assignments. However, at this point, a few students may begin the "creation" phase, with those assigned to storyboard the video presentation beginning their work. Specifically, at this point, a section of the storyboard for the introductory section of the presentation can probably be developed and perhaps several factual sections of the storyboard on general cedar tree populations.

During these middle phases of the process, the teacher will individually be visiting with each student or pair of students working on a particular artifact. A great deal of instructional coaching is done in these individual meetings, where a teacher can inquire about what the artifact is designed to show and thus gauge students' knowledge of the content.

On Thursday, with some members finishing their assigned task for the initial research phase, others would move into creation of their artifacts, working either individually or in small groups. Thus, some students might begin art projects designed to illustrate content, whereas others would continue the storyboard for the video presentation. It might even be possible to begin actual videotaping for the final project. Different students may present different segments of the video related to their work, but not all students have to be pictured in all videos. However, all team members' names should appear in the end credits for any video that is developed, assuring recognition of their individual contributions.

On Friday of the first week, the team should complete the initial draft of the storyboard and continue videotaping. Also, at this point, teachers should meet with each team to evaluate the work and review progress. Either teacher or peer review may be used for this formative evaluation, and any gaps in information can be addressed with additional research. At this time, it may also be advisable to have team members self-evaluate their work, reporting on their progress toward completing their role responsibilities.

On Monday of the second week, videotaping of the storyboard sections continues while other artifacts are nearing completion. The various formative evaluations should be completed if they were not completed on the previous Friday, and from those, the team can determine what additional information is needed.

On Tuesday of the second week, a second research phase begins, based on students filling the "holes" in the presentation by seeking specific information. Individual specifics are added to the storyboard. The video and editing work continues.

By Wednesday of the second week, final additions and revision of the video presentation should be made and all additional artifacts completed. For the cedar tree harvest project, artifacts would include the assigned items presented in the project plan, such as the spreadsheet and the cedar tree count.

On Thursday, the final team meetings would be held. As students gather and review the completed artifacts and videotape, they might note certain things that could be tweaked, and if time allows those changes are undertaken and completed.

Finally, on Friday of the second week, the projects are published via review by all class members. Each team presents their video, and other artifacts, explaining the how and why of their decisions and recommendations. If the teacher chooses, a summative peer evaluation may be conducted for each project as a whole, and at the teacher's discretion, those evaluations may be used as one component of the final grade for the team members. Again, various evaluation and assessment options are described in Chapter 6.

Conclusions

When teachers consider moving toward PBL instruction, it is not at all uncommon to feel a bit overwhelmed. While virtually all teachers have long practiced teaching using the traditional instruction lesson format within unit-based instructional plans, PBL will involve some changes in their instruction, including a loss of some control or certainty as to how instruction may proceed. Thus, some teachers may feel a bit uncomfortable in PBL instruction initially. This chapter has presented rather concrete steps in the PBL instructional process that should help teachers move into PBL with a bit less trepidation.

This is one reason the minilesson was described as one possible instructional option within PBL. Many teachers are more comfortable moving into PBL when they see the minilesson option included in that PBL paradigm, and while many teachers using PBL frameworks conduct no minilessons at all, other teachers may wish to cover particularly difficult concepts using that form of instruction. Certainly, a few minilessons are not incompatible with the PBL paradigm.

Of course, many teachers enjoy interesting challenges and trying new instructional approaches, and they are well advised to experiment with PBL. PBL is frequently discussed as one of the primary instructional paradigms for the future (Barell, 2010; Baron, 2011; Bender & Crane, 2011; Cote, 2007; Partnership for 21st Century Skills, 2009), and certainly the rather drastic increases in student motivation, engagement, and academic performance show that PBL is an excellent instructional approach. PBL also provides many opportunities for differentiating instruction to address the needs of virtually all learners. For that reason, the steps in this chapter should be viewed merely as general guidelines and should not prohibit a teacher from developing PBL units in other, more varied formats. Students are only likely to benefit from teacher creativity in lesson delivery, and nothing herein should stand in the way of teachers and students jointly developing PBL projects as they see fit.

The next chapter will present a variety of technological supports that undergird PBL instruction. In that context, a much longer-term PBL project will be described, with various scaffolded technological supports built into the PBL unit.

4

Instructional Technology in Project-Based Learning Classrooms

This chapter focuses on technology supports for PBL instruction. While a variety of instructional practices are involved in PBL instruction, 21st-century instructional technologies are certainly emphasized within virtually all of the recent PBL literature (Boss & Krauss, 2007; Cote, 2007), and most proponents of PBL have advocated for extensive use of technology in formulation of projects (Boss & Krauss, 2007; Cote, 2007; Laboy-Rush, 2011; Larmer & Mergendoller, 2010; Mergendollar et al., 2007). Some have suggested that PBL must involve in-depth applications of 21st-century technologies and web 2.0 instructional tools (Boss & Krauss, 2007). While that point need not be debated here, most PBL teachers would agree that technology offers many good opportunities for PBL instruction. Further, the technologies available for PBL instruction seem to change virtually every year.

While interactive whiteboards, webquests, wikis, and class blogs as tools for 21st-century education have been discussed since 2005

(Bender & Waller, 2011), more recent social-media applications (e.g., Ning), emerging technological communication devices (e.g., smartphones, iPads), or classroom instructional management tools (e.g., Moodle) now seem to dominate discussions of tech-based instructional innovations. In fact, various proponents of these newly evolving instructional technologies foresee a virtual revolution in the teaching and learning process as a result of these ever-changing technologies (Bender & Waller, 2011, Bonk, 2010; Huber, 2010).

In terms of PBL instruction, the educational technology revolution will probably also involve software presenting authentic simulations to teach content in real-world settings or via videogaming (Eicher, 2010). The relatively recent term "alternate-reality games," or ARGs, reflects the most modern application of simulations for instructional purposes (Stange, 2011). Such games for instruction fit nicely within PBL, as they effectively heighten the engagement of students with the subject matter (Stange, 2011) and add excitement to the PBL project.

This chapter will look at various technology-based instructional options that can enhance the PBL instructional experience, including both commercially available technology or software supports and free online instructional options (Baron, 2011; Bonk, 2010; Cote, 2007; Eicher, 2010). First, some discussion of how modern communication technologies are changing the world, including teaching, is presented, followed by an emphasis on digital technologies that are frequently used in PBL instruction. Next, instructional options for gaming and simulations are presented to show the deep and rich instructional opportunities available in the 21st-century classroom. Finally, a discussion of various instructional approaches such as class blogs, webquests, and wikis is presented, as these innovations greatly enhance PBL instruction.

Teaching in the 21st-Century Digital World

To say that our world is changing dramatically as a result of technology is an understatement. Here is an example. Students at Davis Middle School were participating in a global project following the Space Shuttle *Discovery* as it circled the globe (Ferriter & Garry, 2010). When students realized that the *Discovery* would be passing over an interesting spot on the globe that they had studied (i.e., the Horn of Africa, or the Aleutian Islands), they quickly wrote out a request for a photograph and immediately e-mailed it to NASA. If the request arrived in time and was not lost among other requests for images, a digital copy of a photograph would soon arrive from the *Discovery* for those students. While that alone is amazing to many educators, the students in that project thought nothing of it. Clearly those students were raised in a fast-paced world; in fact, some students found that the photo pages downloaded much too slowly! Of course, their teachers wanted to shout to the rooftops, "You're talking to the Space Shuttle *Discovery* via the Internet—we couldn't have done that when I was a kid! Neither the shuttle nor the Internet even existed!"

While this type of high-interest project is quite exciting to both teachers and students, the truly unnerving thing about this example for veteran educators is that it represents teaching from nearly two decades ago! As Ferriter and Garry (2010) report, this was an example from the mid-1990s! For students today, such instructional examples are merely applications (i.e., apps) of modern technology that can and should be used in school to make the curriculum much more fun and relevant (Frontline, 2010).

Today's Digital World

Students in our classrooms today live in an entirely different world from only five or ten years ago, a digital world of instant communications and amazing command of factual content, often resulting in information overload. To say students today have never known a world without computers is accurate but does not emphasize modern technological innovations nearly enough; specifically, in 2011 as this book is written, the same statement is also true of many early career teachers! Today's students (and many of our younger teachers) have never known a world without the Internet, and modern social networking technologies are commonplace. To put the matter bluntly, being "wired" is today's fundamental life condition.

Today's students and teachers experience a world that is highly connected, completely networked, and increasingly digital. Adolescents and young adults today spend 50 hours or more each week engaged with digital media (Frontline, 2010), whereas only 30 to 35 hours weekly are spent in educational settings (of course, these hours typically overlap to one degree or another). Recently one educator postulated that if students who are so highly engaged with the "wired" world (i.e., the modern digital media world) walked into a classroom that was not wired, the student would experience that classroom as if he or she were walking into a desert (Frontline, 2010). While it may pain many veteran educators, we must consider within that scenario how such a technologically sophisticated student would view some of their more experienced teachers! Because most students today have extensive experience with modern communication technologies, schools simply must adapt by implementing instructional practices such as PBL that use these modern technologies as much as possible, in order to hold the interests of today's preteens and adolescents (Boss & Krauss, 2007; Frontline, 2010).

What Does This Mean for Teachers Implementing PBL?

Technology-based teaching has now gone far beyond software programs as a mechanism to deliver repetitive practice on academic skills (Ash, 2011; Salend, 2009). Today, these instructional options provide actual opportunities for students to collaboratively solve simulation problems and even create content using a variety of options such as wikis, blogs, digital media coupled with smartphones, Facebook, MySpace, and Ning. Students can then publish that information to a worldwide audience via modern technologies, and such worldwide publication is highly motivating to students today (Ash, 2011; Boss & Krauss, 2007, Frontline, 2010). In today's media-rich, high-technology world, effective teachers simply must embrace a wide array of technological innovations in order to reach students at all (Cote, 2007; Frontline, 2010; Partnership for 21st Century Skills, 2007, 2009; Salend, 2009). Fortunately, many teachers have already begun to embrace these options, though others have moved toward technology implementation more slowly. Still, one may well anticipate that virtually all teachers will soon be using these digital technologies, modern PBL software, and other technological innovations for instruction (Cote, 2007; Waller, 2011).

For this reason, the International Society for Technology in Education recently released an updated set of 21st-century technology standards for students to master (www.iste.org/standards/nets-for-students.aspx). These 24 standards include a variety of technology-based skills for the 21st century such as skills for higher-order thinking and general digital citizenship. These include the ability to demonstrate creativity and innovation, communicate and collaborate using 21st-century technology, conduct research and use information or think critically to solve problems and make decisions, and use modern digital technology effectively and productively. Of course, these standards may or may not be included in various state curricular standards, but students must master these technological skills in order to successfully compete in the global economic market of the 21st century. Further, these skills represent exactly those that technology-based PBL tends to develop among students. For that reason, all teachers today should review and implement these technology standards by teaching in a manner that reflects the use of modern technologies. Only by teaching these skills can educators truly prepare their students for the 21st century, and PBL provides an excellent instructional approach for that goal.

Instructional Technology for PBL

While schools vary considerably in terms of the technology supports that are available in the classroom, some consideration should be given to the technologies that can be used to support PBL. While instructional technologies and curricula are rapidly developing and nearly endless, today's classrooms should stress the use of some of the most basic technologies for PBL instruction (Cote, 2007; Davis, 2010; Partnership for 21st Century Skills, 2009; Salend, 2009). While few schools today provide all of these technologies in every classroom, the instructional options discussed here represent a list of desired technology options that will support PBL in virtually any classroom.

Internet-Capable Devices for PBL

Because much of the research in PBL projects is dependent on the Internet, the availability of Internet-capable devices for student use is critical in PBL instruction today. In an ideal world, every student would have an Internet-capable laptop computer for use in both research and presentation of artifacts for the PBL project. Of course, that is a difficult goal to achieve in an era of tight school budgets, and a lack of Internet availability should not prohibit educators from moving into PBL instruction. Specifically, the first PBL instructional project presented in Chapter 1 of this book was not dependent on widespread Internet availability for most of the planned activities. Clearly, in tough budget times, it is not reasonable to hope for either laptops for all students in the classroom or complete Internet availability for all kids in most schools. Nevertheless, PBL instruction will be greatly facilitated with increased Internet capability for the students, which is why some thought as to what Internet availability entails is necessary here.

First, we should note that even in difficult budget cycles, many schools have established full computer availability as a goal, and those schools are attempting to provide a one-to-one ratio of students and laptop computers (Ash, 2011; Frontline, 2010). This is referred to as a "one-to-one laptop initiative." In many districts, parents are encouraged to purchase a laptop, but if that is not possible, the schools provide one (Ash, 2011; Partnership for 21st Century Skills, 2009). Further, the early evidence suggests that computer availability does enhance academic performance, even within lower-achieving schools (Ash, 2011; Frontline, 2010; Manzo, 2010a). One report from the Public Broadcasting television show *Frontline* (2010) demonstrated this effect. Mr. Jason Levy, the principal at a South Bronx middle school (IS 339), initiated a one-to-one laptop program at a lower-achieving school in a rough area of New York City. The school had been characterized by student violence, poor attendance, and little academic success. Mr. Levy and his faculty implemented the laptop initiative in 2004 and soon found that they could reengage nearly all of those students in their school in meaningful learning activities, resulting in a schoolwide achievement increase. Academic score increases of 30 percent in reading and 40 percent in mathematics were demonstrated after laptops were made available, and those educators credited the laptop initiative as the basis for those improved academic scores. They also noted increased motivation and participation in class, improved attendance, and a decrease in discipline problems (Frontline, 2010). Still, this initiative seems to hold tremendous promise for improving academic performance in schools rather drastically, in the same way that modern technologies have improved performance in the workplace.

However, with the recent development of Internet capability via other devices (e.g., iPads or smartphones), availability of a laptop for each student may become less necessary. Any of these devices can provide Internet research capability within a PBL framework. Further, with only several Internet-capable devices per classroom, it is still fairly easy to undertake PBL without one-to-one laptop availability. Here is an example. Within a typical class of 25 students, teachers may create three PBL teams to work independently on the PBL project. Thus, with eight or nine Internet-capable devices, one entire PBL team can do Internet research, while the other teams work on other aspects of the PBL project (organization, digital image development, construction of physical projects, artwork-based artifacts, etc.).

Some schools use portable computer stations called COWs (computers on wheels) with five or six computers, or other Internet-capable devices, on a mobile table that can be moved from room to room. With school budgets quite limited today, schools will certainly need to consider which Internet-capable devices might fit within their budgets and still meet their students' needs. Schools can then carefully marshal their resources over time to provide this Internet availability.

Still, even in poorer school districts, some Internet or computer availability is now the norm rather than the exception, and virtually all educators are moving toward increased use of technology in the classroom. While the actual Internet-capable devices vary over time and from school to school, teachers should note that the Common Core State Standards (www.corestandards.org/the-standards) specifically emphasize use of the Internet in instruction in various standards such as the Grade 9–10 writing standard:

> Use technology, including the Internet, to produce, publish, and update individual or shared writing products, taking advantage of technology's capacity to link to other information and to display information flexibly and dynamically. (Common Core State Standards, p. 99)

To put the matter bluntly, Internet capability, as well as technology-based instruction generally, are critically important for all students today. Internet availability is not only emphasized in modern curricula standards, but it represents best practices for teaching in the 21st century. Technology-based instruction better prepares students academically, and this trend toward increased technology-based instruction will certainly facilitate an increasing emphasis on PBL instruction. Again, states such as Texas that did not adopt the Common Core State Standards still have technology standards within their curriculum, as shown in the appendix.

> Teachers should have access to six to eight Internet-capable devices in every classroom when moving into PBL.

Presentation Software

Because many of the artifacts that result from PBL instruction involve digital images, digital graphics, and highly developed multimedia presentations, both teachers and students will need access to modern presentation software such as PowerPoint (Salend, 2009; Waller, 2011). In modern instruction, both teachers and students should be routinely developing various presentations using such software to aid comprehension of the material and in the creation of persuasive arguments on the class content. Also, once an effective presentation is developed, either by the teacher or by students, that topical presentation can easily be stored in digital form for future use. Modern presentation software is designed in a user-friendly fashion to allow for use by students in virtually all grades, and students as young as Grade 1 or 2 are developing PowerPoint presentations across the nation today (Bender & Waller, 2011). These media-savvy skills will clearly be in demand in almost all 21st-century jobs (Partnership for 21st Century Skills, 2007; Salend, 2009). Again, within the context of PBL instruction, schools can easily teach these modern presentation skills.

Interactive Whiteboards for PBL Presentations

Many classrooms today are equipped with interactive whiteboards or similar devices. These are electronic, digitally interfaced presentation boards that allow presentation of the contents of the computer screen on the board for the entire class, and they serve as replacements for the older chalkboards or dry-erase boards of yesteryear (Marzano, 2009; Marzano & Haystead, 2009; Salend, 2009). These presentation options also allow instruction to be much more interactive, as teachers and students can create interactive lessons requiring students to make choices on the interactive whiteboard itself, compile data on the opinions of class members, or present PBL project artifacts to the entire class. When a PBL presentation is undertaken, the whole class may participate by viewing the bullet points as well as any digital images, video segments, or other PBL artifacts.

Like the laptop initiative discussed earlier, research has shown that interactive whiteboard technology leads to increased academic achievement. For example, Marzano's recent research has documented significant increases in academic achievement, ranging from 13 percent to 17 percent, when interactive whiteboards were used as an instructional medium in the classroom (Marzano, 2009; Marzano & Haystead, 2009).

> Interactive whiteboards allow PBL projects to be displayed classwide and tend to increase academic achievement.

Digital Video Cameras

Another technology frequently used in PBL projects involves capturing digital images, either still photography or video, in order to supplement PBL projects (Cote, 2007; Salend, 2009). While pulling relevant images off the Internet to construct project artifacts is quite common in PBL projects, creation of one's own images within a PBL project is more exciting for many students and allows for much greater publication options, as copyrights for images are not involved. Also, modern digital video cameras are not terribly expensive and will enhance many of the artifacts to be developed within the PBL projects, particularly if a given project is to be presented to a committee or governmental body as one of the publication options. Within the context of a PowerPoint presentation, digital images or video will improve the overall look of the artifact and increase the persuasive impact of that artifact. For that reason, use of digital cameras should be facilitated and encouraged in PBL projects.

Students generally enjoy assignments that involve creativity more than drill and practice–types of assignments, and in particular, students enjoy developing digital videos that will be published in some format (Salend, 2009). Further, the skills involved in developing a cohesive video include many organizational skills that are used in effective writing. For example, storyboarding a video is very similar to outlining a written theme, and writing skills (e.g., scripts for video segments) are frequently necessary in developing videos. One might well argue that the English and language arts curriculum of the 21st century should include these video development and persuasive presentation skills, as well as the more traditional outlining or persuasive writing skills. Certainly the availability of a digital video camera will enhance students' preparedness for the 21st century.

Simulations and Games for PBL

With that list of desirable hardware in mind, teachers should also consider what software can enhance the PBL instructional experience for the students. Obviously software that directly parallels the desired learning outcomes should be sought and incorporated into the PBL unit, and with the continuing enhancement of modern instructional software, virtually all teachers can find some gaming or simulation software for use in the PBL units. Further, all teachers should be using these modern teaching tools; the use of gaming and simulation software is expressly stipulated as a recommend 21st-century teaching standard by the International Society for Technology in Education. In the ISTE standards one can find the following standard:

> *Use models and simulations to explore complex systems and issues.* (www.iste.org/standards/nets-for-students.aspx)

Today, the purest examples of complex problems and issues for use in PBL instruction may be found within technology-based simulations and games (Ash, 2011; Laboy-Rush, 2011; Satchwell & Loepp, 2003; Stange, 2011). Parents and teachers have long realized that students across the age span play modern digital games by choice, often for many hours each week. The game Civilization, as one example, has been available for many years and may be one of the most common as well as one of the most popular instructional games on the commercial market (Stange, 2011). Both Civilization and a similar game, Age of Empires, involve having students build civilizations within various historic time periods, including planning for such concerns as food sources for the growing population, public health, overall happiness of the population, production of trade goods, protection from enemy civilizations, and the important relationships among the development of food sources, population growth, and trade.

Clearly these games are teaching and reinforcing some of the big ideas from the social studies curriculum on the development of civilizations, and they are teaching those ideas within games that students enjoy. In that sense, tying instructional content to such simulations and games has been a common practice at least since 1990. Further, using project-based gaming and simulations for teaching educational content is not only effective as an instructional approach, but it is one of the most effective ways to quickly engage students' interest (Ash, 2011; Satchwell & Loepp, 2003).

However, with today's technology, the available gaming and simulation options are nearly limitless. Teachers are well advised to consider all available games and simulations in their content area, as well as reflect on the types of activity that might engage students' interest (Ash, 2011; Stange, 2011). Further, as the technology for games and simulations continues to evolve, this instructional approach is being tied to current educational issues. For example, Tabula Digita is a set of immersive, educational video games that can be used in middle and high schools for teaching mathematics within the framework of the recent response-to-intervention initiative nationally (Eicher, 2010). The games in that curriculum include a wide range of mathematics skills from computational fluency and mathematics concepts through problem solving. This program has been used to teach mathematics, ranging from basic instruction for all students to assisting students struggling with mathematics.

Perhaps an example would best illustrate the advantages of using games and simulations for instruction within the classroom. Imagine that one is teaching a unit on the late antebellum period and the Civil

War. In that unit, some attention would be given to the Underground Railroad that assisted slaves in their attempts to escape into freedom. Teachers can teach that content in a variety of ways including the following:

- Assigning students to read a section on the Underground Railroad in the text;
- Having students view a video about Harriet Tubman and her activities along the Underground Railroad; or
- Having students engage in a simulation in which they become escaping slaves, moving along the Underground Railroad in the 1850s. In that scenario, the students (i.e., slaves) that escape to Canada with their families win!

Given those instructional options, teachers should reflect on which teaching techniques are likely to engage students' attention more. One might well argue that all of these techniques could be used to teach this content, and certainly that is true, but most educators would agree that the simulation would help students to feel and sense the reality experienced by those enslaved persons much more so than the other, more traditional instructional approaches. In short, simulations and games work so well in teaching simply because they are much more engaging than more traditional instructional methods for today's learners (Ash, 2011; Laboy-Rush, 2011; Stange, 2011).

To teach the reality of slavery, teachers might consider a simulation called Flight to Freedom (http://ssad.bowdoin.edu:9780/projects/flighttofreedom/intro.shtml). This simulation was designed to help students experience the struggles of slaves in the antebellum South who tried to escape into freedom in Canada. Thus, this simulation activity fits nicely into instructional units on the antebellum period or the Civil War.

The game can be played individually or in small groups of students and is intended for students from the mid-elementary through high school grades. The player (or group of players) is initially presented the opportunity to choose one of nine actual characters from the antebellum period (e.g., Sojourner Truth, Frederick Douglass, Harriet Tubman, etc.). At first, the player will read a paragraph-long biography of that character, and thus the instructional content of this game reinforces the history curriculum. Then the character is placed randomly somewhere in the southern states and presented with both a status board (indicating overall health and financial resources) and a description of the situation in which the character finds himself or herself.

The student's character then has to make choices (try to escape from here, remain here and wait, or seek news of one's family). The object of the simulation is to get oneself and as many family members as possible into Canada in order to escape slavery. Of course, each move one makes holds consequences for the character in terms of costing money or damaging one's health if sufficient food is not found. At the end of the game, students are "scored" by how many of their family members are then traveling with them toward Canada and how many moves they took to reach their goal.

Like most simulations, this game could be used as an adjunct to the class in order to help students sense the overwhelming odds against escaping slaves. While text and video segments can and should be used to teach this same content, students are much more likely to sense what those persons actually felt—what they actually went through—when they are confronted with the same types of choices that were faced by escaping slaves (e.g., remain in this barn another day, go out and try to purchase or steal food, run away, or hide). Further, this type of gaming scenario, like all project-based learning, will result in much higher levels of engagement and, thus, in higher mastery of the content.

ARGs in the Classroom

Today, however, simulations and games are no longer tied to computers in the home or classroom. Rather, modern alternate-reality games (ARGs) are web-based, computer or mobile phone–enabled games for teaching content and increasing student engagement. Most ARGs are highly interactive and require students to engage in various activities in the real world in order to compete with each other, either individually or in teams, while completing the game. In most ARGs, students receive clues for the activity and other instructions, as well as feedback, during the gaming activity itself. While the current technology for ARGs is only in its infancy, educators have begun to experiment with ARGs in the classroom, and this exciting technology application can lead nearly anywhere. Increasingly teachers are exploring these technologies for instructional purposes.

ARGs weave together real-world information and artifacts using clues and puzzles hidden within an alternate reality housed within the websites. The artifacts under study in the ARG might come from any online library, museum, store, or website or may involve using recorded messages or media such as movies, television programs, and printed materials. ARGs typically invite players to meet and talk with characters in the narrative and jointly use various online resources to complete the puzzle or task as they learn about the topic in general. Further, ARGs are not merely information delivery systems. In fact, Stange (2011) described several modern gaming simulations that not only teach academic content but also involve students directly in the production of content.

ARGs often blend factual information with fictitious characters played by the students, as the students complete missions within the game. For example, a recently created ARG called Pheon (www .pheon.org), developed by the Smithsonian American Art Museum, was launched in the fall of 2010. Pheon is a mission-based ARG that employs the tried-and-true gaming plan of the classic game Capture the Flag. Thus, Pheon is a team competition in which the game's virtual talisman, the pheon, seeks to restore balance to a virtual world called Terra Tectus. Players choose teams and then complete various missions involving the museum's art collections and online exhibitions in order to earn points and complete their missions. Pheon can be played on site, online, or in a combined fashion for students who live near the museum.

This game also requires students to complete tasks such as taking pictures of specific artifacts that in turn help them solve puzzles to complete their missions. They will be learning about the art during the game as they explore the Smithsonian collection online. One activity in Pheon requires players to take a digital picture of their favorite tree and post that to the gaming website with information about it. Not only do the students thus pick up some information on trees in that activity, but those pictures are then included in a massive online catalogue of biological species called the Encyclopedia of Life. That is a multiinstitutional project intended to create a digital archive of every species on earth (Stange, 2011). Thus, by participating in this ARG, students are not only passively learning but are also actively contributing to online content for the various agencies compiling that encyclopedia. This phenomenon is referred to as curatorial "crowd sourcing," and in that process, virtually anyone and everyone can become a museum contributor!

While ARGs represent a very recent trend, they will be appearing in classrooms in the near future, and teachers should understand that ARGs are currently being used in education on a limited basis. For example, one use of virtual reality for teaching was recently explored by Harvard University where an alternative-reality 3-D environment is currently being used to teach a law course. That environment is known as Second Life (www.secondlife.com). When one joins Second

Life, that person creates an "avatar" or digital self who, within the environment, is given the option of constructing buildings, buying land, creating schools, or any other physical spaces that come to mind. Other avatars that appear in one's Second Life world are other persons that are being controlled in real time by someone else on the Internet. Thus, all teachers should get a sense of what alternative reality might do in education by reviewing the seven-minute video on using Second Life in education (http://edupln.ning.com/video/uses-of-second-life-in).

Using the Second Life environment, various higher-education institutions have begun to formulate online learning options. Both Ohio State and Harvard University have participated. As one example, a faculty member at Harvard Law School recently presented a course on "Law in the Court of Public Opinion." Thus, using the virtual-reality format, students wishing to have a true Harvard experience may use that 3-D environment to audit the course and study a university course for credit in an alternative reality featuring buildings that resemble the actual ones on the Harvard campus (www.pbs.org/teachers/learning.now/2006/10/cyberone_the_future_of_educati.html). One can only imagine where the ARG phenomenon might take educators within the next five to ten years, but this can and probably will become a powerful tool for proponents of project-based learning.

Accessing Simulations for Your Classroom

Many simulations and project-based learning scenarios in a wide variety of grade levels and subject areas are available either for a small fee or are entirely free online. The TechTrekers website (www.techtrekers.com) presents a catalogue of hundreds of teaching games and simulations that teachers can use immediately in the classroom in virtually every curricular area. While most of these are focused on middle and high school grades and relate to content areas in mathematics and science, many social studies games and simulations are also included, as are games in a variety of other content areas. Teachers should spend some time checking on the links at this site, since many of those simulations can be used within ongoing instructional units.

For example, Online Math Applications is intended as a set of supplemental activities for Grades 5 through 8 that encourages middle school students to apply mathematics to real-world simulations, including music, history, science, and travel examples.

In contrast, the site also presents more complete project-based simulations that are intended to actually replace the curriculum for a period of time. Mathematics Modeling, as one example, is intended for Grades 11 and 12 and designed as a semester-long web-based course in mathematics modeling. Box 4.1 presents a few descriptions of games, simulations, and links that are presented on the TechTrekers website.

Box 4.1 Games and Simulation Learning Websites

Adventures of Jasper Woodbury. This program provides simulated real-world problems in mathematics and mathematical reasoning developed by the Cognition and Technology Group at Vanderbilt University in the early 1990s.

Aha! Science (Grades K–5) and *Imagine Mars* (elementary and middle school). These are simulations that encourage students across the ages to explore science and in particular, to imagine planting a colony on Mars (www .thelearningcompany.com).

Amazon Interactive. This scenario, intended for Grades 3 through 12, places students in the Amazon to study the geography and peoples of that region. In particular, students will explore the life of the Quichua tribe as they live off the land.

Flight to Freedom. This game helps students understand what enslaved persons experienced as they sought to escape to freedom in Canada during the antebellum period (http:// ssad.bowdoin.edu:9780/projects/flighttofreedom/intro .shtml).

The Fractals. This site helps students in Grades 9–12 explore fractals.

Fractals Exploration. This is intended for Grades 11 and 12 and presents fractals from the Mandelbrot set and Julia sets.

The Hot Seat. This gaming scenario places students in the "hot seat" during a job interview setting to give practice in landing a job.

(Continued)

Box 4.1 (Continued)

Mock Trials. This was developed by a law firm and presents a mock trial with sons and daughters of employees on the *Titanic* who are involved in a lawsuit on responsibility for that shipwreck.

Nature Virtual Serengeti. This simulation experience allows students to experience an African safari through virtual reality (www.xpeditionjonline.com/09vsserengeti.html).

Tabula Digita. This is an immersive educational video game for teaching mathematics in middle and high schools within the RTI framework. It includes problem-solving skills, computational fluency, and key mathematical concepts (888–982–2852 or www.DimensionM.com).

TechTrekers. This website (www.techtrekers.com) presents a catalogue of hundreds of teaching games and simulations for middle and high school classes that teachers can use immediately in the classroom.

Whyville. This simulation (www.whyville.net) allows students to create an artificial world, with all the problems and concerns of real-world nations. For example, in this web-based game, the programmers chose to introduce a systemwide infectious disease ("Whypox") without letting the student players know it was coming. Thus, like the Centers for Disease Control and the World Health Organization, the students playing Whyville have to contend with a totally unanticipated disaster and still build their civilizations.

WolfQuest. This game, created by the Minnesota Zoo, allows students to learn about wolf ecology by exploring Yellowstone National Park (as a wolf!).

The Learning Company

Many commercial companies provide games and simulations for virtually any topic taught in the public school age range. For example, several curricula are offered for elementary grades in STEM (i.e., science, technology, engineering, and mathematics) by the Learning Company (www.learning.com), and most of these include various simulations and games that can be incorporated into project-based learning. All of their curricula are presented in a digital teaching environment, and students can proceed at their own pace in most of these activities. However, all of these curricula also provide for hands-on instructional activities that the teacher can use as minilessons for the whole class within the PBL framework.

For example, Aha!Science is a supplemental science curriculum for kindergarten through Grade 5 that focuses on key concepts in science. The modular design of this curriculum allows teachers to extract portions of the curriculum for use, and various instruction modules, lesson plans, and quizzes are presented for either supplemental intervention activities or enrichment. Games and simulations within the curriculum give students the opportunity to apply the scientific method through practice in engaging, real-world settings. Online journaling is one feature of this curriculum that facilitates students' reflections on science on an ongoing basis.

In particular, this company provides an online PBL simulation in science called Imagine Mars in which students complete a project to create a life-supporting community on the planet Mars (Laboy-Rush, 2011; information on Imagine Mars is also available on the Learning Company website). In that PBL unit, students will have to reflectively consider what constitutes a successful community on Earth, research the conditions on the surface of Mars, determine what is needed to survive there, investigate resources of Mars that might help sustain the community, and ultimately create community models for Mars that are then shared. In one study, students using this simulation-based PBL unit demonstrated increased scores in mathematics and on scientific process skills for problem solving (Satchwell & Loepp, 2003).

Aha!Math is another curriculum provided by this company. This curriculum is built on the curriculum focal points of the National Council of Teachers of Mathematics and is likewise aligned with the Common Core State Standards in mathematics and various other state standards (e.g., the TEKS standards from Texas). There are more than 400 curriculum assignments ranging across 19 instructional units. Because this is presented in a digital environment, individual students will receive exactly the instruction they need in a differentiated instructional framework, and students can progress at their own pace throughout most of the instructional units (with the exceptions of the games and simulations). The instructional units from kindergarten through Grade 2 consist entirely of games and simulations, while the units from Grade 3 through Grade 5 are framed in instructional modules complete with activities and quizzes, as well as a variety of games and simulations.

Conclusion: Games and Simulations in PBL

As this discussion shows, newly evolving games and simulations promise to greatly enhance all instruction, but they are particularly applicable within PBL instruction as both instructional formats focus directly on high levels of student engagement. Teachers exploring PBL should consider the use of various games and simulations and seek free resources on the Internet for the PBL projects.

Technology-Based Instructional Options for PBL Instruction

In addition to games and simulations as instructional tools, many other instructional options have recently evolved and are frequently incorporated into PBL projects. These include the use of webquests, class blogs, wikis, and social networking within the classroom. While these instructional options may be likewise used in traditional instruction, they are particularly appropriate in PBL projects, as they greatly facilitate a new teaching and learning process. As discussed in Chapter 1, both these technology-based instructional innovations and PBL in general attempt to change the teaching/ learning dynamic from a teacher-driven lesson with the student as the passive recipient of instruction to a more dynamic and engaging student-driven exploration and problem-solving process in which the teacher facilitates learning that students choose to undertake (Bender & Waller, 2011). This changing instructional dynamic probably accounts for the higher levels of student engagement in PBL instruction, and it is certainly a hallmark of PBL discussions in the literature (Barell, 2010; Baron, 2011; Cole & Wasburn-Moses, 2010; Drake & Long, 2009; Grant, 2010; Larmer & Mergendoller, 2010; Maloney, 2010).

Given the extremely limited time teachers have for learning new techniques, the instructional options discussed shortly were selected because learning these techniques is fairly easy. Teachers who have not used technology a great deal in their teaching previously can, with relative ease, develop and use blogs, webquests, or wikis for instruction as discussed. Therefore, these ideas might represent one way for teachers who previously have not been technologically oriented to move toward teaching 21st-century skills in the classroom.

Webquests Within PBL Projects

While webquests have been used in education since approximately 1995 (Salend, 2009), many teachers might be unfamiliar with them because of limited Internet availability in their school. Essentially a webquest is a research assignment that is typically given to individuals or small groups of students that requires searching the World Wide Web seeking information about a particular topic (Skylar, Higgins, & Boone, 2007). Webquests, such as the example in Chapter 1, are typically guided by specific questions, assigned tasks, or issues that are identified by the teacher and involve students seeking specific information on a particular topic (Okolo, Englert, Bouck, & Heutsche, 2007; Skylar et al., 2007). Students follow links that have been identified and reviewed by the teacher as holding specific information necessary for project completion. Also, most webquests include some options for student choice, and suggestions for additional, less structured explorations of the Internet, that should result in additional information to enhance the final webquest assignment.

> A webquest involves students following Internet links identified by the teacher in order to answer specific comprehension questions about a particular topic.

Most webquests are basically similar and typically include a variety of components such as the following:

an orientation or introduction with background information,

specifics on the required tasks for students to accomplish,

the processes students should undertake including recommended links to explore,

a list of resources or links to check for information,

an evaluation mechanism that clearly states expectations, and

a method to summarize the experience.

To illustrate these points, a sample webquest for an upper elementary or middle school history class is provided in Box 4.2. Note that this webquest ties the content on the Civil War to many previous events such as the Missouri Compromise of 1820, the *Dred Scott* decision, and the Nullification Crisis of the 1820s.

Box 4.2 A Sample Webquest on the Civil War

(Recommended for students in Grades 5 through 9)

Webquest Questions: What were the major causes of the Civil War? Did the Civil War impact our sense of federal authority versus state authority? Does this question still baffle our nation today?

Initial Assignment: Working in pairs, students will complete each of the following required assignments on the Internet by writing your answers down to the questions at each site. Students may also complete other searches on related topics and use that information to answer the questions. Each answer should be at least a paragraph in length.

I. Link I Assignment:

(www.visit-gettysburg.com/the-battle-of-gettysburg-timeline .html)
(http://americanhistory.about.com/od/civilwarmenu/a/ cause_civil_war.htm)

1. At these two sites, look at the events that are mentioned as causes of the Civil War. What events are linked to the beginning of the Civil War by the author/creator of the visit-gettysburg.com site?

2. What is the Missouri Compromise? When was it repealed? How was it related to the Civil War according the author/ creator of the visit-gettysburg.com site?

3. What is an abolitionist? What impact do you believe the *Dred Scott* decision had on abolitionists in the northern states?

4. Given the causal events presented in the timeline on the visit-gettysburg.com site, what is the major cause of the Civil War?

5. Does the other website listed present other causes? Should these have been reflected on the timeline at the visit-gettysburg.com website?

(Continued)

Box 4.2 (Continued)

II. Link II Assignment:

(http://answersinhistory.wordpress.com/2007/01/06/the -nullification-crisis/)

1. What is the Nullification Crisis? What two sides were in conflict and why?

2. What issues were represented by the two sides in the Nullification Crisis?

3. Do those issues reflect the issues that later led to the Civil War?

4. Is the issue of states' rights versus federal authority a possible cause of the Civil War?

III. Required Additional Link:

Each pair of students is required to identify at least one additional web link that presents information on the causes of the Civil War. After reviewing information on that link, students must likewise provide specific instructions on which part of the link they reviewed (i.e., how to get to what they viewed) and three questions that other students should be able to answer after reviewing that link.

Hints:

Use Google Maps to review some of the major battlefields.

Select a video from YouTube on causes of the Civil War.

Identify recent news articles that discuss the causes of the Civil War.

Review the Wikipedia information on the Civil War. Is there information from your work that could be added to Wikipedia? Discuss any additions with your teacher.

(Continued)

Box 4.2 (Continued)

IV. Culminating Assignment:

After most pairs of students have completed Assignment 1, the teacher will place you into six larger groups, with three to five students in each group. The task for each of the larger groups will be to design a five-minute digital video segment related to the causes of the Civil War. The specific topic selected by each group and the storyboard for their video must be approved by the teacher in advance.

Reflection Questions to Address in Your Video:

Use the following questions for both reflection and as a basis for some of the information included in your presentation.

1. What issues have been considered causes of the Civil War during the last 150 years? Have perspectives about the causes of this war changed?

2. Are various advocacy groups today still debating the cause(s) of the Civil War? What positions do these groups take?

3. From 2011 through 2015, Americans will remember the various events in the Civil War, as those years represent the 150th anniversary of the entire war. What would you recommend as an appropriate remembrance of this seminal event in American history?

In this webquest, more advanced students may be required to complete all of the tasks, whereas students with more limited academic skills may complete only the first three activities. Also, this webquest is initiated as a peer partner activity, and that partner activity will assist students in staying on task during this work. This particular webquest culminates in the development of a multimedia project, which may be one artifact required in a larger PBL project in the American history class.

Teachers should note that in this webquest, elements of the Common Core State Standards are obvious (the relationship between this assignment and Texas standards is described in the appendix). While many Common Core State Standards across grade levels could be related to items in this webquest, the notations that follow should suffice to show that webquests can address the Common Core State

Standards with relative ease. These notes use the notational format from the Common Core State Standards (www.corestandards.org/the-standards). For example, the following Common Core State Standards are addressed by the first assignment as well as the multimedia assignment within this webquest. Further, many other Common Core State Standards could be listed here, since they are addressed by other sections of the webquest.

> *RH.6–8.7. Integrate visual information (e.g., charts, graphs, photographs, videos, or maps) with other information in print.*
>
> *RL.4.9. Integrate information from two different texts . . .*
>
> *RL.4.2. Compare and contrast firsthand and secondhand information . . .*
>
> *SL.4.2. Add audio and visual displays to enhance the ideas and themes . . .*

Finally, in addition to relating webquest assignments and artifacts to specific Commmon Core State Standards, the provision of the rubric for evaluation of the webquest will assist students in understanding their task. Rubrics help students structure and plan their work and ultimately determine when their work is completed. Thus, rubrics help students focus their time and energy during the webquest and will typically result in a better overall product. Box 4.3 presents a sample rubric for the Civil War webquest.

In order to maximize student engagement and motivation, webquests should be specifically designed with both research and fun in mind. Webquests should focus on interesting sites and require more than merely answering questions at those sites. They should feature sites that present video segments, animation, sound, maps, photos, or other types of digital media. Also, as students identify additional websites related to the topic at hand, teachers may review information on those sites and ultimately incorporate them into future webquests on the same topic. In that sense, student research on the web can greatly benefit teachers developing webquests on a particular topic.

Building a Webquest

Building a webquest does take some time, as teachers should initially find links and develop specific questions or activities for students to complete at those links. While merely using a website to answer questions on a research topic is certainly appropriate in webquests, identification of links that require students to actually do something should also be included. This might involve having students take a quick quiz on the topic or complete a personal inventory on their feelings or opinions relative to the topic. This type of web-based activity

Box 4.3 A Rubric for Evaluation of the Civil War Webquest

Evaluation	Indicators	Grade
Poor/adequate	All nine of the initial questions were answered. One additional website was identified. A presentation was completed that adequately addressed each question.	D
Good	All nine of the initial questions were answered. Two or more additional websites were identified. A presentation was completed that addressed each question.	C
Very good	All nine of the initial questions were answered, with careful consideration of alternative answers evident. Four or more additional websites were identified, and questions were developed that could be used to assist future students with their studies. A presentation was completed that addressed each question and posed other thoughtful questions.	B
Excellent	All nine of the initial questions were answered, with careful consideration of alternative answers evident. Four or more additional websites were identified, and questions were developed that could be used to assist future students with their studies. A presentation was completed that addressed each question, posed other thoughtful questions, and was constructed in a creative manner.	A

will typically result in higher levels of student engagement. Finally, while activities should be varied, the guiding questions should focus directly on the topics to be mastered. Both teachers and students may develop these questions, and again, student research on the web can be very helpful in developing and improving previously developed webquests. A variety of websites are available that can be used by teachers in developing webquests, as presented in Box 4.4.

Box 4.4 Websites to Assist in Developing Webquests

www.Internet4classrooms.com/using_quest.htm. This website describes five components of webquests including introduction, task description, process for completion, evaluation criteria and rubrics, and conclusion. Additional links are provided for development of webquests.

www.kn.pacbell.com/wired/fil. This website offers free templates for creating webquests. Step-by-step instructions make it fairly simple for teacher use.

http://questgarden.com. This website was created by Bernie Dodge, the developer of webquests. This site does require membership, which costs $20 for a two-year subscription. The site offers user-friendly templates for creating webquests and makes it easy to upload documents, images, and worksheets in the webquest. It also encourages users to share their work. Instead of creating a completely new webquest, teachers can use previously designed webquests and adapt them for their individual needs. A 30-day free trial is available if teachers are interested in sampling the website before subscribing.

https://www.teacherweb.com. TeacherWeb is another online tool that helps create webquests and web pages. The subscription costs $27 annually.

webquest.org/index.php. This website provides links to several short videos that describe development and use of webquests in education from a faculty member at San Diego State University. There are options for finding existing webquests in a variety of topics and also for developing webquests on your own.

www.zunal.com. This website is another webquest maker that does not require a subscription.

As webquests vary considerably in complexity, there is some difference of opinion on the relationship between webquests and PBL instruction, as discussed in Chapter 1. Some webquests may, in fact, represent PBL projects in and of themselves, whereas others that are more limited in scope are best considered components of a larger PBL project. This book presents a number of webquests that should be considered components of PBL projects, since in the view of this author, PBL is much more than merely a webquest. However, as an example of a webquest that could represent a complete PBL project by itself, teachers should review a webquest on the Civil War that has been used by teachers in Hawaii for several years at the following website: http://kms.kapalama.ksbe.edu/teams/kauila/civilwar/civilwarprocess2005.html.

Clearly, webquests vary considerably in the level of structure that may be provided, and therefore, this instructional idea provides teachers with an opportunity to differentiate their webquest assignments. Teachers may differentiate by providing more detailed instructions on the webquest for students that require more guidance and offer less structure for other students. Also, a variety of optional links and associated activities may be provided. This distinction between required and optional links allows groups of students to individualize their webquest and pursue subtopics within the overall topic that may be of particular interest to them (Cote, 2007). In those webquests, once the required links are reviewed and the assignments for those links completed, students may be encouraged to explore the broader topic on their own by finding other Internet-based information.

Some teachers design several versions of the same webquest, with the various versions based on students' ability, learning style, interests, and reading levels. Students with highly developed reading and technology skills can be given additional links to higher-level reading material on the content, while students needing more assistance might have links to lower-level reading material specifically aimed at their reading level. One website allows teachers to test the readability of other websites, and using this site prior to designing a webquest will assist the teacher in developing a webquest that meets the needs of all of the students in their classes (see http://juicystudio.com/services/readability.php#readweb).

> Students with highly developed reading and technology skills can be given additional links to higher-level reading material on the content, while students needing more assistance might have links to lower-level reading material.

There are many advantages to using a webquest in the context of PBL instruction. Webquests are highly versatile and may be completed in the classroom, in computer labs, in the media center at the school, or at home (Cote, 2007). Thus, even if Internet capability is limited within the classroom, use of webquests within a PBL unit is possible based on Internet availability elsewhere in the school or home. Further, webquests represent authentic learning in that these searches help students learn about various 21st-century technology applications (Cote, 2007). Virtually all students in the elementary grades and higher have already used Internet search programs in their personal lives, and teaching them how to appropriately use the web is a critical 21st-century skill.

Also, webquests provide an excellent opportunity for the teacher to teach critical information evaluation skills. Unlike school textbooks, which have been evaluated by experts for accuracy, as well as approved by state curriculum committees, information on the Internet is completely uncensored, and much of it is inaccurate or misleading. Thus, webquests provide an excellent opportunity to teach important information evaluation skills, such as detecting the difference between fact and opinion or determining an author's purpose in writing the information found on the Internet. In an era of total information overload, retrieving appropriate, topical information and evaluating it for accuracy is paramount. Box 4.5 provides a series of questions that students may be taught to consider when obtaining information from the Internet. Teachers are encouraged to use these questions and add to or edit them in any way needed to make them more appropriate in their classroom.

Box 4.5 Evaluation of Information From the Internet

Information obtained from the Internet, like all information, must be evaluated to determine its usefulness in proving a point or defending a position on a topic. The 12 questions below will help you consider how you might evaluate information from the Internet, and these questions are also helpful in evaluating information from all news or other sources.

1. Is the position of this author stated clearly and succinctly? Is there ambiguity in what the author is trying to say?

2. What is the source of the information you are using? Is this from a website (if so, remember to copy down the entire website as your source)?

3. Is this website a reputable news source or another type of Internet source (e.g., such as someone's blog)?

(Continued)

Box 4.5 (Continued)

4. Is the information credited to or cited from another source? If so, is that a reputable source?

5. Is evidence provided to support the author's position on this website? What is the quality of that evidence? How many separate evidence-based points does the author make to argue for his or her position?

6. Are there counterarguments that you've found elsewhere that were not addressed here? If so, can you have confidence that the source that omitted those arguments is believable?

7. Is the evidence believable? Is the overall position of the author believable? This is sometimes called the "smell test," which means essentially, does this person's perspective or argument stink too much to be believable?

8. Are all sides of the issue discussed fairly? Are there sides of the issue, question, or topic that are not represented in this work?

9. Is the author of the work identified? Does that author have a particular perspective that you can identify? Is that author open and honest in presenting his or her perspective, and does that perspective lead to overt bias in the work you are using?

10. Have you identified other sources that present the same ideas? Is there a consensus on the issue or topic you are studying that you can identify?

11. Is an expert opinion or perspective presented? If so, who is the expert, and does his or her expertise relate directly to the question at hand?

12. Is celebrity endorsement used in this work? What value can you ascribe to that endorsement? Does the celebrity have celebrity based on an area of expertise directly related to the topic?

Like the webquest itself, the skills involved in the evaluation of information correlate well with many of the Common Core State Standards. For example, the following Common Core State Standards are clearly represented within various indicators in Box 4.5 (see the appendix for comparable standards from Texas):

RH.6–8.1. Cite specific textual evidence to support analysis of primary and secondary sources.

RH.6–8.6. Identify aspects of a text that reveal an author's point of view or purpose (loaded language, inclusion or avoidance of particular facts).

Classroom Blogs in PBL Projects

While webquests can be quite exciting as research tools, they are similar to research done via more traditional educational endeavors such as the use of books or libraries. Webquests, like research projects based on encyclopedias or texts, involve students fundamentally as static learners or consumers of existing information, rather than as active creators of information or problem solvers. In contrast, classroom blogs offer teachers the option of having students actually create content as they complete assignments online in an environment in which all class members can see and review each other's work.

A blog is an online journal or discussion in which participants post their contributions to various questions under study (Salend, 2009; Waller, 2011). In the PBL context, teachers may wish to create a blog either to cover factual content or to discuss the deeper, conceptual questions related to the content under study. Blogs can be limited to students in one PBL group or can allow students from various PBL groups to participate in the discussion by adding comments to various postings of others. All blog entries by either teachers or students are catalogued and become reading or study materials for others on the blog. Various blogging websites allow students the opportunity to connect with teachers and other students worldwide for interactive discussions on almost any topic whatsoever. Some of these websites are presented in Box 4.6.

Box 4.6 Websites for Creating Class Blogs

www.21classes.com. This is another blog option for teachers that offers several layers of protection for students in the class, including password protection and additional teacher controls. A free version is available as well as a fee-based version that offers higher levels of security.

www.classblogmeister.com. This free website provides a template for teachers to create their own password-protected classroom blogs.

(Continued)

> ### Box 4.6 (Continued)
>
> **www.edublogs.org/why-edublogs.** This blog-hosting website provides guidance for blogs in education at all grade levels.
>
> **www.gaggle.net.** Gaggle provides free or fee-based e-mail and blog tools for teachers and students. The site has numerous filters available that allow teachers to screen inappropriate terminology and provides adequate controls over those posting on the site.

Blogs can provide many types of educationally based social interactions in education (Boss & Krauss, 2007). For example, Davis (2010) reported that students were using blogging to ask questions to both the teacher and to other students about algebra homework in one high school in North Carolina. Students answered each other's questions and, in many cases, saved the teacher considerable time. Manzo (2010) reports that the interactive nature of blogging can be quite motivational for many students, and many teachers have found blogging to be a powerful incentive for students to read more in the content areas, particularly among lower-level readers. Blogs allow for connections between students in the same class, the same school, or with students in classrooms halfway around the world, and some of the most interesting blogs in education involve long-distance contact. Imagine a class studying the American Revolution in Arkansas discussing that period of history with a class in Great Britain!

> Many teachers have found blogging to be a powerful student incentive to read more in content areas.

Rather than have students post on public blogs, some teachers choose to use a secure blog that is specific to their classroom or school. These blogs are typically established within the context of a single school or single class, and this generally provides an added degree of security for the students, since secure blogs are password protected. In these blogs, the content is monitored and controlled by the teacher.

In short, blogs provide a 21st-century option to have students socially interact with the content under study, and as such, students are typically highly motivated to study using this instructional tool. This also is a relatively simple way for teachers with limited technological skills to begin to use web 2.0 tools in their classroom. Finally, blogging fits nicely into the broader PBL paradigm, since both content and social interactions are emphasized when the class is blogging together.

Using Wikis for PBL Projects

As noted, blogging does involve the potential for more active student participation in learning. However, today many teachers are moving beyond blogging and have now undertaken the use of wikis in the classroom because wikis, unlike class blogs, offer greater opportunity for students to work together. Rather than merely commenting on each other's work, wikis allow students to actually work together by editing each other's work. Thus, wikis encourage collaboration in the creation of content as students explore their research topics together (Bell, 2008; Fernando, 2007; Rowen, 2005).

Most teachers today are familiar with a commonly used wiki, the online encyclopedia Wikipedia. That wiki includes entries on virtually any topic one can imagine and is entirely created by users who are allowed to edit any entry in the encyclopedia and, thus, change the content. This encyclopedia may include some inaccuracies on specific topics, but given the high number of users, those inaccuracies are typically corrected very quickly by other users worldwide.

A wiki in the classroom would work in the same general fashion. Using a wiki in the class, students can creatively write about any general topic on the wiki, edit work that other students have put on the wiki, develop a digital video and upload it to the wiki, or prepare a document, with all students editing the work of their peers. A wiki is, essentially, a private or semipublic website created by either the teacher or the students that includes content addressing a specific topic (Waller, 2011). Text, pictures, and virtually any digital media may be included in the wiki, and wikis allow the opportunity for students to both critique and edit each other's work (Bell, 2008). Wikis are now used widely in industry as one way to have employees collaborate on large, difficult-to-solve problems. For example, the U.S. Army used a wiki in Afghanistan to compile geographic and other information that was useful to the troops in that conflict (Bell, 2008).

> A wiki is, essentially, an intentionally constructed website created by either the teacher or the students that includes content addressing a specific topic.

In the classroom, the option of collaboratively generating and editing information results in increased excitement for learning. In fact, when students realize that their work will be published on the wiki page, it encourages them to spend more time developing their ideas (Bell, 2008; Rowen, 2005). Wikis may be published in a range of accessibility, from available only to designated wiki members (i.e., students in a given class and their teacher) or publicly available for everyone on the Internet. Like other modern technologies, wikis result in students creating content rather than passively reviewing it, and that is one great advantage of using wikis in education (Rowen, 2005; Waller, 2011).

Wikis in the classroom provide educational options that were not even possible only a decade ago, and teachers are embracing this technology, since students enjoy this newly evolving type of socially based learning. In addition to collaborative creation of content, most classroom wikis offer teachers a variety of other options. First, virtually any digital media (e.g., pictures, video, charts/tables) can be imported for students to use. Next, most wikis provide an option for teachers to review the history of entries in the wiki (Bell, 2008). Using that function, teachers can see which students made specific content contributions at what times. This can provide one option for grading student participation in wikis. However, many teachers choose an alternative; they require participation on the wiki, but they do not grade it because unpacking a complicated history log for 25 different students making multiple entries on a class wiki can be quite cumbersome.

Finally, creating a wiki is fairly easy. Several websites provide an option for teachers to create a wiki at no charge for educational use (http://pbworks.com or www.wikispaces.com). These wikis typically include all basic wiki functions and can be mastered by novices in around 30 to 45 minutes.

There is considerable variation in how wikis might be used in the classroom. Some teachers use a wiki for each PBL project during the academic year. Others have chosen to create one classroom wiki and continue to build on that single wiki throughout the school year. This can be done fairly easily by providing additional pages for vocabulary terms, concepts, or digital demonstrations for each separate instructional unit or each PBL project during the year. Also, the content that teachers develop for wikis can easily be transferred from one wiki to the next if teachers are teaching the same or similar content during years. Box 4.7 presents a description of a wiki that might be used for a PBL project in social studies, history, or a history/social studies/English block class.

Examples of Wikis in the Classroom

Here are several examples of other wikis recently developed in a workshop conducted by this author at Hapeville Charter Middle School in Atlanta, Georgia. Mr. Michael Phelps is a science teacher at Hapeville Charter Middle School during the school year. During the summer, he is a tornado tracker; he runs a business chasing tornados and providing exciting photography on tornados to various media

Box 4.7 Description of a Wiki on the Civil War

1. Use video segments when you can. The wiki should focus students' interest on the topic at hand, and digital photos or video segments are an excellent way to do that. YouTube and TeacherTube are excellent places to find videos to introduce your wiki. Of course students will access numerous video segments during this PBL unit, but because the wiki tends to be one of the initial required tasks in the PBL unit, an overview type of video segment is preferable here. This author would recommend something like what is found at this website:

   http://kms.kapalama.ksbe.edu/teams/kauila/civilwar/
   civilwarprocess2005.html

   Using that site, I'd use a few lines of the wiki to suggest that students spend 5 to 10 minutes, working in pairs, clicking through the website process and the student work. It is advantageous to show students excellent work by other students, since this often will motivate them to work harder. Using student work from that PBL webquest project is one way to do that.

   (As a sidenote, this author would suggest that each reader review the student work button for 2007 and specifically the song summarizing the Battle of Kennesaw Mountain. I personally live near that battlefield and have toured it many times. In a brief video segment, these students from Hawaii sing a song they wrote that accurately describes the Union attack on June 27 at Kennesaw, the commanders of each army in that battle, and the fact that the Confederates beat the Union troops back down the mountain. Providing students the opportunity to publish that song worldwide is great teaching!)

2. Present an organizational paragraph. After students have spent some time on those video segments, teachers should present a paragraph on the home page of the wiki describing what the wiki will be used for. Here is a sample.

   (Continued)

Box 4.7 (Continued)

"The Civil War was a defining event in American history, and many of the issues and disagreements represented by the two sides in that conflict continue to impact our history today. This wiki will present various views of that conflict, as well as some opportunities for you to express your informed opinion on the issues and questions that were resolved, or remained unresolved, from that war. This wiki will continue to grow as we construct information about the causes of the war, the conflict itself, and the issues that surround the war."

3. Next, if websites can be found where students actually "do" something other than merely view information, I'd include those on the home page of the wiki. For the Civil War, there are various quick-quiz opportunities available on the Internet (simply Google "Civil War quiz"). At many of those sites, students can take quizzes to measure their initial understanding of the war. I'd suggest this site:

   *http://history.howstuffworks.com/american-civil-war/
   civil-war-quiz1.htm*

4. After those three items (webquest done by other students or other video segment, the introductory paragraph, and the quick quiz) are presented on the home page of the class wiki, I'd suggest the teacher "lock" that content to prevent students' editing. Students will be invited to edit other sections of the wiki, but not that introductory page content.

5. Teachers should immediately create some information for students to add to or edit the wiki. Because teachers in virtually all subject areas teach vocabulary related to individual units in their subject, a vocabulary page provides an excellent initial opportunity for students to add content to the wiki and edit each other's work. Prior to introducing the wiki, teachers should create a vocabulary page, add their vocabulary terms without definitions, and have students provide those definitions in the wiki.

(Continued)

Box 4.7 (Continued)

6. Because video segments provide a good instructional option for teaching content, and emphasize 21st-century communication skills, I'd recommend that teachers begin a third page in the wiki for student-created video segments. Making a digital video camera available is critical, but students can add content to the wiki in a number of ways, such as the following:

- Writing a one-act play with a Union and a Confederate soldier discussing their view of the reasons for the war
- Staging a "press interview" with a student playing the role of either Jeff Davis (Confederate president) or Abe Lincoln discussing their view of the reasons for the war
- Having General Robert E. Lee (Confederate commander in Virginia) and General U. S. Grant (Union commander) discuss why they prosecuted any of the battles where they were in command against each other
- Having Harriet Tubman (a former slave who helped other slaves escape to freedom) debate President Jeff Davis on the meaning of the Civil War for America

outlets (www.stormscapelive.com). During a recent workshop on PBL instructional techniques, Mr. Phelps created a wiki on tornados, completing the initial work in approximately 35 minutes. On the home page of his classroom wiki, Mr. Phelps included several pictures he had taken of tornados that were already on his website. He also included some introductory information about the purpose of the wiki, about tornados in general, some directions for students on how to edit various pages in the wiki, and a few thought-provoking questions for students to consider. Finally, on his wiki homepage, he listed several introductory websites for students to look over. Using the functions within the wiki, Mr. Phelps then "locked" that page to prevent editing that specific content.

Next, to facilitate student participation, Mr. Phelps created another page within that wiki that included vocabulary terms on the topic. He invited his students to participate in the creation of those definitions, so he didn't lock the vocabulary content on the second wiki page. He wanted his students to provide definitions of those terms and edit each other's definitions. Using just that simple wiki, Mr. Phelps will essentially have students "teach" the vocabulary content of the unit to each other via that editing function, and he will not have to spend class time doing so! He'll be using that wiki during the next school year.

Many other instructional ideas were generated by teachers in that workshop. One teacher had, with her students, completed a PBL project in ecology the previous year. That project involved transforming a simple grassy space on the school campus into a green space/ garden with selected plants, a bench, and a walking path. Students selected the flowers, trees, and shrubs for the green space based on climate, availability of sun (since the grassy area was partially shaded), and average rainfalls. That teacher felt that a class wiki would be a great place to publish the results of that previous PBL project including before and after digital photos of that space. Next year, she might have students develop a video guide to the plants that were planted in the garden.

Another teacher in that workshop developed an interesting idea for using a classroom wiki in sixth-grade mathematics. He began to create a wiki on solving mathematics problems. He realized that he provided the same explanations year after year for various types of problems (e.g., instructions for solving for an unknown variable in the equation $3x + 5 = 29$). By creating a digital video explanation describing the steps involved in solving that problem, he could place that short video on his class wiki and use that for either initial instruction or review on that type of problem. Further, he also planned to use several of his more advanced students to develop digital videos on solving other types of problems. He can thus have some students make the videos as a class project, and after review of that content, he can include the additional videos in his class wiki.

In each of these instances, the teachers had not used wikis previously in their instruction, though some were more advanced in using technology than were others. For example, Mr. Phelps already had a company website with many photos and videos of tornados that were appropriate to include in his wiki, whereas the mathematics teacher had never considered using wikis previously in teaching. Still, all of these teachers were able to initiate a wiki and begin planning additional wiki pages, and additional uses for their class wiki, after only 45 minutes or so of practice. Because of the intuitive nature of wikis, and the relative ease of wiki development and use, this author encourages all teachers to consider this technology as one 21st-century teaching option. Many websites are available to assist, and some of these are presented in Box 4.8.

> ## Box 4.8 Wikis in the Classroom
>
> *http://ethemes.missouri.edu/themes/1246.* This site provides a list of other sites that can assist in the development of wikis or understanding how wikis may be used in the classroom.
>
> *www.iste.org.* This is the website for the International Society for Technology in Education. This is a member-supported nonprofit group dedicated to effective use of technology in PK–12 classrooms as well as in higher education. The organization provides 24 standards for students to master, and while specific technologies such as wikis are not mentioned by name, they are included in the overall discussions.
>
> *http://legacy.teachersfirst.com/content/wiki.* This website includes information on how to create a wiki for classroom use.
>
> *http://wikisineducation.wetpaint.com.* This site has extensive information about wikis. It is a fee-based service, but it is quite popular with teachers and includes a number of videos developed by users.
>
> *www.wikispaces.com/content/wiki-tour.* This website provides a video tour that describes using wikis in the classroom. It is a good introduction for teachers.

Khan Academy

Since 2010, the Khan Academy (www.khanacademy.org) has provided an impressive and powerful instructional option that is free to students and teachers worldwide. This website is dedicated to anytime/anywhere learning and provides specific instructional lessons on virtually any topic one can imagine. Many of those instructional lessons are coupled with video demonstrations that show the problem's solution. In short, this is a resource that can and should be used by virtually every teacher worldwide.

During instruction, teachers often present the same solution steps to particular types of problems at various times during the instructional unit. While this has always been the case throughout the history of education, having teachers present the same explanation or demonstration of a problem multiple times during an instructional unit is not an efficient use of the teacher's instructional expertise. Fortunately, modern technology offers another option—video demonstrations of various types of problems coupled with various types of educational exercises. This is what Khan Academy provides worldwide. Further, these exercises and video demonstrations are coupled with several methods for tracking students' progress (e.g., a knowledge map showing students where they are, what they have accomplished, and what they should do next) and for providing reinforcement for problem completion (i.e., badges for various levels within the online curriculum).

Khan Academy's website uses a gaming instructional format to encourage students to enjoy reading, social studies, science, economics, astronomy, and mathematics. Initial development was completed by a teacher in California, Sal Khan, and today that work has been scaled up rather dramatically and is partially funded by the Bill and Melinda Gates Foundation. In short, Khan Academy provides virtually an entire public school curriculum ranging up through high school and college-level work, and it is entirely free! The website can be used by individual students who progress through their studies at their own pace, or it can be used by a teacher's entire class. The site challenges students to move as far as they choose to in the content, and when students experience difficulty, they can access 2,700 video demonstrations on the specific content they were studying. For example, in mathematics, the videos include demonstrations of problems ranging from 1 + 1 through calculus. All of these video demos can be viewed as is, and each breaks down particular content into easy step-by-step instructions. Students can use these individually, or working in pairs, to solve a particular problem.

Various tracking features allow teachers to follow the progress of both individual students or their entire class, and anecdotal teacher testimony suggests that many students get so excited using Khan Academy (based on their option of earning reinforcement badges for achievement) that many progress way past their current grade level. In the context of a PBL project, students can seek clarification of various points necessitated in development of project artifacts using Khan Academy rather than seek information elsewhere. In that sense, the Khan Academy provides an excellent resource for all teachers and in particular for teachers implementing PBL.

Social Networks: Twitter and Ning in the Classroom

Imagine teaching a class in which every student is actively engaged in learning, in which every single student is actively participating in class discussions and collaborations related to the content. For many teachers that is a potent, powerful image, and of course, it is one major goal of PBL. Like PBL, modern networking options hold the promise of extremely high levels of student engagement, and for that reason, social networking should be considered as an essential component of PBL in the 21st century.

Throughout this book, we have discussed the popularity of social networking among students today (e.g., Facebook, MySpace, Twitter). As noted previously, the average teenager spends more than 50 hours weekly engaged with digital media, and the majority of that is spent in social networking (Frontline, 2010). In some schools, educators have reported to this author that virtually every student is engaged with one of these social networking sites, and some teachers are struggling with students texting and networking during class. How many teachers have found themselves saying, "Put down your smartphones, and let's get to work!"

Rather than fight that battle for student attention, many teachers across the grade levels have begun to incorporate social networking technologies into their instruction, whether or not they move immediately into PBL. These teachers have developed various ways to use social networking options in education, particularly within PBL, since PBL projects tend to involve high levels of collaborative work anyway. As one example, some teachers have begun to have students BYOT (bring your own technology; e.g., Internet-capable laptops, smartphones, iPads, etc.). For students without personal Internet-capable devices, teachers make classroom computers available, often pairing students. Then in classwide discussions, minilessons, or PBL team discussions, students can use Twitter to "tweet" their answers to the teacher's computer, and using the interactive whiteboard, those answers can be shared with the entire class.

Many teachers have begun using Ning to facilitate that social-learning collaboration in the classroom (www.ning.com). Ning is a fee-based social networking site that, while not exclusive to education, can be implemented as a social networking option for an individual classroom. Ning allows teachers (or anyone) to set up a social network and begin the social interaction that is so critical for teaching students today. Once a Ning network is set up for the class, teachers then use this network for discussions of various topics or for creating collaborations among their students.

Ning social networks have been used by teachers as well as administrators, parents, and students as communication tools or supplements for the curricula, allowing educators to share teaching ideas and best practices. Recently Ning announced a partnership with Pearson Education to provide Ning networks free for kindergarten through Grade 12 educators in the United States and Canada. The Ning Mini is an option to provide education-based networks for up to 150 members, coupled with a whole set of online collaboration tools such as blogs, photos, and forums (http://go.ning.com/pearsonsponsorship/).

Of course, neither Ning nor any social networking tool should be considered essential in PBL, but many teachers have begun to use social networking such as Ning networks as components of PBL projects.

Moodle

Moodle is a fee-based course management system designed to assist teachers and students develop and formulate their own Internet-based courses or websites (http://moodle.org/about). It is much more extensive than the wikis described earlier but often includes wikis and the other technology-based instructional tools described herein. "Moodle" is an acronym for Modular Object-Oriented Dynamic Learning Environment, and the use of Moodle has become popular among teachers who wish to create web-based content associated with their courses. A worldwide network of teachers using this system has grown considerably since its inception in January 2005, and there are presently 35 million users at more than 50,000 locations around the world. In 2010, Moodle 2.0 was launched, and it incorporates many more features that teachers requested, making this a highly effective, well-regarded course platform.

Like the other technology and ideas in this chapter, PBL instruction is not dependent on Moodle. While PBL instruction can certainly be based within a Moodle, this brief discussion is presented simply because teachers may see this term in the literature on PBL or educational technology for the future.

Technology for Publication of PBL Projects

In addition to the instructional options already noted, modern communications technologies offer many opportunities for publication of student work. Publication may involve placing one or more artifacts from a PBL project online or placing an entire PBL project on a website where it can be viewed and reviewed by others. Chapter 1 presented a variety of publication opportunities ranging from placement of an artifact in a local newspaper to presentation of PBL project findings to a government board or commission. Again, knowing that their work might be viewed by a fairly large audience does tend to motivate students to do their best work (Drake & Long, 2009; Grant, 2010; Larmer & Mergendoller, 2010; Marzano, 2007), and technology-based publication options, like more traditional publication options, factor in to that motivation.

For digital files (e.g., text, photographs, audio recordings, or video), the Internet provides a variety of publication options. Publication may be as simple as placing the PBL artifacts on a school or school district website, which typically allows all students, teachers, and parents to view that work. Further, because most school websites are not restricted to local users, placement of a PBL artifact or a PBL project on a school website really represents worldwide publication of that work. Still, other publications options may provide more visibility for PBL projects because many open-source Internet locations include search functions that might direct viewers worldwide to the published material. Here are a few publication options to consider that seem quite motivating to students.

> Publication may be as simple as placing the PBL artifacts on a school or school district website, which typically allows all students, teachers, and parents to view that work.

YouTube

YouTube (www.youtube.com) is a collection of professional and amateur videos that are posted free online. While not intended for education, many teachers today are using some of these videos as an instructional tool by publishing student work from PBL projects in this forum. As an instructional tool, teachers are increasingly finding that many of the videos on YouTube can be beneficial after a careful review by the teacher. In fact, it is quite common for teachers to download YouTube videos on specific topics to their class wiki, since such videos can be excellent additions to the anchor for a PBL project. Most YouTube videos are from two to five minutes long, though longer ones are also plentiful, and teachers can find videos on many topics covered in public school classes. Further, as a publication opportunity, YouTube provides teachers and students the option of making their PBL work available digitally in a much wider forum than a school website.

Teachertube

TeacherTube (www.teachertube.com) is a site similar to YouTube, except it is specifically intended for educational use. It includes an array of short videos that can be used in instruction, and while the collection of videos is not nearly as extensive as YouTube, TeacherTube does include a large number of videos on various topics. With a quick scan of the most frequently viewed content on June 7, 2011, this author noted videos on the following topics:

• Dividing fractions	• Space Shuttle	• Combustion of iron
• Perimeter rap	*Endeavor* launch	• Literature circles
• Great quotes	(2011)	• Fifty nifty United
	• Multiplying	States
	fractions word	
	problems	
	• American	
	Revolutionary War	

While a search of these videos is not guaranteed to produce a video that is useable in the classroom, many such searches do, so like the YouTube site, TeacherTube can offer teachers and students opportunities to seek information for introducing or completing their PBL project, and both sites certainly provide opportunities for publication of student work.

Student Security, Media Security, and Media Literacy

When one considers publication of student work in any forum, student security becomes an issue. Of course, student safety and security is a critical concern for parents as well as every educator in the 21st-century classroom, and as the learning experiences migrate increasingly to PBL and the other Internet-based learning environments described here, issues of security become even more critical. Further, when students are publishing pictures of themselves, as they occasionally will in digital video files within various PBL projects, security is paramount.

Naturally, security and personal responsibility go hand in hand on the Internet, as elsewhere, so instruction for students on their digital security and instructional or personal use of the Internet, as well as their social networking, is paramount. In that sense, security in the digital world involves the issue of media and technological literacy (Bender & Waller, 2011). Students must be taught how to seek, develop, evaluate, and interpret information found on the Internet, and because that environment is totally unregulated, educators must address security and appropriate use of these new technological opportunities (Partnership for 21st Century Skills, 2007, 2009).

When planning activities such as webquests, YouTube publication of PBL projects, or Ning social networking within the class, careful guidance for students is in order. Teachers should begin with careful website selection. Previewing website content is always in order, though students will certainly access and obtain information from a variety of sites that teachers have not previewed. Initially, school faculty should develop policies on Internet usage, if such policies are not already in place. These policies should stipulate personal responsibility for students to immediately exit inappropriate websites, as well as whom they should notify if they find themselves at an inappropriate website. All teachers should regularly discuss with students what types of sites are appropriate for use in schools and what sites are not.

Of course, no information about students or student contact information should ever be posted on open blogs or publicly available websites. In fact, absolutely no student addresses, personal e-mails, phone numbers, or any other personal contact information should ever be posted in the digital environment. Student pictures should only be posted in groups, or when students are working on various PBL activities, and teachers should review those prior to posting them. In many schools such student projects may only be posted after parental permission has been obtained, while other schools secure each year a rather "open" permission for posting students' projects. Also, in any videos that might be uploaded to the web, students should be encouraged to use only first names. Of course, no student should have an online profile posted on the classroom blog, or class website, unless secure classroom-only or school-only sites are used.

When considering these security issues on the Internet, teachers should actively teach these precautions to their students. This may also include cautions relative to posting any private information not only on school-related sites, but also on social networking sites such as Facebook and MySpace. While those sites are generally not related to school endeavors, and should generally not be used for school activities, a discussion of the cautions that apply for any posting of personal information is certainly appropriate in today's world.

A Sample Technology-Based PBL Project

While many other examples could be provided of technology that can enhance PBL-based instruction, the ideas just presented should help teachers initiate their technology-based PBL project. To summarize these technologies, a PBL project in a middle school social studies class is presented here. It may be instructive to compare this project with the project presented in Chapter 1, noting the increased application of modern instructional technologies in this project. Box 4.9 presents a sample PBL project, Planning a Civil War Memorial Garden, which represents an opportunity for an upper elementary, a middle school, or even a high school class to assist the community in commemorating local history.

This PBL project is quite extensive and might be used in various subjects such as English, history, or social studies while studying the Civil War and time period. This covers U.S. history from 1820, the date of the threatened succession of South Carolina in the Nullification Crisis, until 1877, the end of reconstruction period. This PBL project might also be used in a block class combining history, social science, biology, and English skills. A project of this nature represents a longer time frame (perhaps nine weeks to a semester long), but teachers should note that the content of this project does incorporate an extensive time frame within a U.S. history class. Also note the student choices provided in the assignments section involving development of various artifacts or completion of different assignments. Student choice of this nature typically results in more enthusiastic participation in the project.

Conclusions

This chapter has presented only a few of the simpler technology instructional applications that can enhance PBL instruction, and teachers are certainly encouraged to explore a more expansive use of technology as their time and school district resources allow. To restate an ongoing theme, PBL instruction is not dependent on extensive use of technology, and teachers are well advised to explore problem-based instruction regardless of the availability of technology in the classroom. When preparing for teaching in the 21st century, sooner is better than later, and teachers must move quickly toward PBL.

With that noted, judicious use of modern instructional technologies will greatly enhance the PBL learning experience, and thus, use of technology is certainly warranted in PBL instruction. The cojoining of PBL and technology has greatly increased learning opportunities

Box 4.9 Planning a Civil War Memorial Garden

Project Anchor

The city of New Bern, North Carolina, is planning an extensive memorial for the Battle of New Bern of 1862. A portion of the battlefield has been purchased, and a small museum dedicated to the Civil War has been constructed on that land, and it is now open to the public.

The Battlefield Commission has requested detailed plans and suggestions from the public on how to plan a half-acre garden that will remember and honor all participants, both Union and Confederate, with North Carolina connections from those troubled times. In particular, the Commission notes the following as points to honor and memorialize in that small garden.

1. The North Carolina 26th Infantry defended the Confederate position that is preserved on the battlefield, with great honor and courage. That group was a locally formed infantry unit of North Carolina men, and many students in that locale today may find ancestors (or at least individuals with the same surname as their own) in that unit. Other Confederate units included the North Carolina 7th, the 35th North Carolina, and the North Carolina Confederate Militia. These other units may be mentioned in the recommended memorial, but that is not a requirement.

2. New Bern was the location of the Trent River Camp, a settlement of escaped or newly freed slaves, and their struggles to escape to freedom should be remembered and honored in this garden.

3. The African Brigade of New Bern was formed in the Trent River Camp shortly after that battle. It was made up of former slaves from the New Bern area of North Carolina who chose to fight with the Union for the freedom of other slaves. The African Brigade was thus made up of local men and must be honored in this garden space. While many Union units from other states fought or were stationed in New Bern during the Civil War, none of the other Union units was made up predominately of North Carolina men. These other Union units may be mentioned in the plans, but that is not a requirement.

(Continued)

Box 4.9 (Continued)

The task and challenge for any group or school class that wishes to participate is to develop plans for an appropriate half-acre garden, including a monument or monuments to honor all of these persons, as well as remember their historic, though different, perspectives on the Civil War. The Commission is highly sensitive to the conflicting opinions on the causes of the Civil War and what should and should not be celebrated, so they require that any project recommendations demonstrate deep awareness and sensitivity relative to these complex issues.

In the James City Middle School, the seventh-grade students in a history/language arts block class (third period) have chosen to undertake this as a PBL project from September through October of the academic year.

The Driving Questions

- Can one garden location next to this new museum serve as a remembrance for these diverse groups?
- Should perspectives of persons in history that have been rejected by modern society (e.g., the perspective of southern slave owners who may have fought in the Confederate units) be honored today? Can one develop an appropriate remembrance for their bravery and sacrifice and yet not honor a cause (i.e., slavery) that has been rejected by recent history?

The Project

Present specific recommendations, costs analyses, and design ideas for the half-acre garden memorial to the important citizens of New Bern and North Carolina who were involved in that conflict. These should be provided to the Battlefield Commission no later than November 30, 2012. This project will be undertaken within the history/language arts block class period, with some involvement of the science teacher relative to appropriate memorial plants and recommendations on the memorial garden. In the history/language arts class, three PBL groups will be formed, and each will work independently on this project.

(Continued)

Box 4.9 (Continued)

Topics of Study

- Nullification Crisis
- Major battles in North Carolina (New Bern, Fort Macon, Bentonville, Fort Fisher, Plymouth)
- The Missouri Compromise
- The *Dred Scott* decision
- Other events leading to the Civil War
- The Underground Railroad
- The current debate on causes of the Civil War
- Important persons (Abe Lincoln, Jeff Davis, Harriet Tubman, Frederick Douglass, Sojourner Truth, generals Robert E. Lee, U. S. Grant, William T. Sherman, Joe Johnson)
- Important battles in other states during the Civil War (e.g., first and second Bull Run, Shiloh, Gettysburg, Vicksburg, Petersburg, the Atlanta campaign)
- The Freedman's Bureau

Required Activities, Artifacts, and Grading

All student PBL groups must complete assignments numbered 1, 2, 4, 5, 7, and 8, and the culminating project assignment. However, each PBL group may choose to delete two of the assignments from the following set: 3, 6, and 9. All grades will be combined by the teacher into a number ranging from 0–100, and scores on that scale will be averaged for each student in order to generate a final semester grade. However, the grade for the culminating project will be counted twice in the final grade calculation; thus, that grade holds twice the weight of other grades on the assignments that follow.

1. Students working in pairs will complete three of the following webquests. Rubrics are provided for each of these webquests, and these will be graded by the teacher. On the webquest, partners will receive the same grade.

   — Causes of the Civil War (presented earlier)
   — Presidents from 1820 to 1877

(Continued)

Box 4.9 (Continued)

— Critical battles of the war

— Westward expansion and slavery

2. All students will complete a jigsaw study of major North Carolina battles that impacted the Civil War. Jigsaw groups will take a quiz on this information, and the group with the highest average score wins a pizza party for their group, to be arranged by the teacher.

3. All students will be required to participate in the class wiki on the Civil War (as described earlier). Students are expected to use that wiki in developing their ideas for the recommendations on the half-acre garden design, as well as complete all other work. Also, all students are required to develop definitions of terms related to the Civil War and other events in American history that are on the class wiki. Student participation will be evaluated via written notations from the teacher, based on the number of wiki entries and the overall factual and conceptual quality of those entries.

4. Students will individually keep a reflective journal in electronic form (using Word) throughout the project. These should reflect your thoughts on the life-changing questions and issues that various persons experienced throughout this period, with particular attention on the subject of your biography (described in the next assignment). These journal entries will not be graded but will be read by the teacher, and in some cases, certain journal entries may be shared electronically with other class members.

5. Students, working independently, will research a specific important person of their choice and write a bio of that person (a minimum of five pages). They may choose from the list provided or select another person (with teacher approval). No two students in the PBL group will study the same person. A rubric has been provided for the development of this biography. These will be graded by the teacher and then placed on the class wiki upon completion.

(Continued)

Box 4.9 (Continued)

6. Each student will be required to play the Flight to Freedom game (described previously in this chapter). Students should reflect on that game in their journals, with particular attention to any North Carolina connections or locations involved in the Underground Railroad.

7. Each student will produce or participate in the production of a minimum of one creative product (e.g., a one-act play, a staged debate, a PowerPoint presentation, a puzzle or game, or other type of creative product) focused on major conceptual questions such as, "What is the impact of the Civil War on American history?" These will be finished products ready for publication in some appropriate venue (these may overlap with other assignments on this list). Each product will be shown to the class and evaluated by others in the class in conjunction with the teacher. Only students working on a particular creative product will receive the grade for that product, but all students in the class must participate in the creation of a minimum of one creative product.

8. Each PBL group will develop two planning artifacts: (a) a time line of events for the eight weeks of this study, including specific goals projects must attain, and (b) a list of individual assignments for each group member. This time line and assignment of specific tasks will be required by the end of the first week of the project. These are nongraded assignments.

9. Each PBL group will provide a detailed memorial garden diagram as part of their recommendation for the half-acre garden, along with descriptions of any monument(s) to be placed there. A budget for development, landscaping, recommendations for monument(s), appropriate plants, sitting areas, walking areas, and other designated areas will be developed. This is due by the end of the sixth week of the project time line, and a rubric has been provided for evaluation of this plan. The entire class, using that rubric, will evaluate these artifacts. Each member of your group will receive the same grade on this artifact.

(Continued)

Box 4.9 (Continued)

Culminating PBL Project

The Battlefield Commission has invited our class to make a complete recommendation for an appropriate half-acre garden memorial, and these presentations should reflect and include many of the artifacts listed, as determined by the PBL group and the teacher. This recommendation will be presented as both a PowerPoint presentation and a set of hard-copy designs for the memorial garden to the commission. The design recommendation, if accepted, will be presented in the local media for comment. The teacher will award the final grade for the culminating project, and each member of your group will receive the same grade on this artifact.

(Boss & Krauss, 2007; Larmer et al., 2009; Salend, 2009), and this cross-fertilization promises to continue for at least the next decade. Of course, many teachers today are struggling to not be left behind in this rather drastic transition to technology-based instruction (Bender & Waller, 2011), and continued improvement in their technology skills will better prepare them for teaching in the classrooms of the future. In fact, many educators believe that this represents a rather drastic change from traditional instruction as practiced in the 20th century, and even simple technology applications (e.g., use of webquests or wikis in the classroom) can move a class in the right direction (Bender & Waller, 2011; Bonk, 2010; Huber, 2010). With that in mind, teachers are well advised to explore any of these technological innovations they can and begin to implement these in their classes as soon as possible. This clearly facilitates PBL instruction and is in the best interests of all of the students in the class.

5

Instructional Strategies in Project-Based Learning

While the recently evolved technology-based teaching tools discussed in Chapter 4 will, of necessity, force many educators to learn several newly evolving instructional skills, other instructional strategies that are frequently described as essential components of PBL are not as new. For example, cooperative learning is often mentioned as an essential component of PBL (Schlemmer & Schlemmer, 2008), and that instructional tactic has been used in classrooms for the last three decades. Thus, teachers may be much more familiar with this instructional option than with many of the newer technology options. Proponents of PBL typically recommend extensive use of cooperative group-work because cooperative tasks reflect the types of demands of the 21st-century work environment more so than individual problem-solving tasks (Bender & Waller, 2011; Partnership for 21st Century Skills, 2009; Schlemmer & Schelmmer, 2008). For that reason, teachers should maximize cooperative tasks within the overall PBL project.

Other strategies that are frequently described as components of PBL might include brainstorming, grouping students for instruction, student-directed inquiry tactics including various metacognitive instructional procedures, and teacher-directed instructional tactics such as scaffolded instruction (Barell, 2007, 2010; Boss & Krauss, 2007; Larmer et al., 2009). Again, while many of these strategies are not particularly new for many teachers, this chapter presents overviews of these instructional practices, as they might interact to form a viable, real-world PBL experience. Further, PBL tends to result in the use of these strategies more frequently or in slightly different and creative ways in the classroom. Therefore, this chapter presents a discussion of both student-directed inquiry strategies and teacher-directed instructional strategies for PBL. Instructional tactics dealing specifically with the evaluation of assignments and grading of artifacts within a PBL project are discussed in the next chapter.

> Proponents of PBL typically recommend extensive use of cooperative group-work because cooperative tasks reflect the types of demands of the 21st-century work environment more so than individual problem-solving tasks.

Within this broader discussion of instructional strategies for PBL, one overriding theme that all teachers should note when they consider the PBL framework is the changing role of both the teacher and the student (Larmer et al., 2009). In PBL, teachers become instructional facilitators rather than instructional leaders or content delivery persons. As discussed in the previous chapters, teachers will need to learn several new skills for instructional facilitation in PBL instruction or more fully develop their skills in this relatively new instructional area. For example, while many teachers have included student projects in the curricular expectations, including student projects that reach beyond a single unit of instruction (e.g., the yearly science project requirement), basing the entire curriculum or a substantive portion of the curriculum on a project-based learning experience is quite a bit more involved than those more traditional individual project assignments and will still demand new skills.

The starkest example of this changing teacher role might be the role of a secondary social studies teacher who, rather than delivering a lecture or leading a whole-class group discussion on a topic (i.e., the traditional instructional leader role), now has a much more instructional-facilitative role. For that teacher, this new role might include the following:

- Assuring that text, Internet, and other resources are available on the student-chosen driving question;
- Suggesting various community persons that might be interviewed on a given topic;

- Locating videos in the media center;
- Presenting options for student-planned time lines and other supports for student planning of various aspects or artifacts within the PBL project;
- Facilitating PBL group discussions and brainstorming on the topic;
- Providing minilessons on specific aspects of the chosen topic or problem;
- Coaching individual students or small groups on group working, cooperative learning skills;
- Evaluating assignments, both individually (i.e., the traditional teacher evaluation role) and by using teacher evaluation coupled with student evaluation; and
- Any other type of coaching, cheerleading, counseling, and arbitrating authority to settle disputes.

In terms of the new role for students, PBL instruction will demand many skills that are not highly stressed in more traditional instructional paradigms. Like the traditional teacher described earlier, students in traditional classrooms may have received some practice in these skills, but PBL will result in increased demand for these student-directed learning skills. These include the following:

- identifying and selecting critical questions and problems;
- brainstorming novel solution options for selected questions or problems;
- working cooperatively with other students;
- crafting evaluation comments for the work of other students that both compliment and show deficiencies in that work; and
- determining the overall worth or value of the various contributions of other students.

As these lists indicate, both teachers and students will need to master many new and innovative instructional roles and skills. Thus, teachers should note that, within PBL, student and teacher mastery of these skills is considered critically important. First, a discussion of student-directed inquiry skills is presented, followed by a discussion of instructional tactics used by teachers within PBL. This discussion includes both newly evolving and more tried-and-true instructional strategies that facilitate PBL.

Student-Directed Inquiry Skills in PBL

Within a PBL framework, students are directing much more of their instructional time than in traditional classes. Therefore, students will need planning and time organizational skills, cooperative learning skills, and many other skills for successful participation in PBL classes. In one sense, the emphasis on these skills is a strength of the PBL approach, as self-directed inquiry results in more independence in learning and, typically, higher levels of participation (Barell, 2007). In fact, proponents of PBL instruction have often noted that these new learning roles of students more appropriately represent the skills needed in the 21st-century workforce than traditional classroom learning skills (Barell, 2007; Partnership for 21st Century Skills, 2009; Schlemmer & Schelmmer, 2008). However, for students who have not been exposed to PBL, teachers will need to provide some instruction on this set of learning and organizational skills. It is not appropriate for teachers choosing to implement PBL to assume that students know the requisite skills for PBL instruction. Rather, students must be initially taught a range of new learning skills such as those noted shortly.

> Within a PBL framework, students are directing much more of their instructional time than in traditional classes so they will need planning and organizational skills, cooperative learning skills, and many other skills for successful participation in PBL classes.

Finally, while the teacher must lead in the early instruction of these skills, students will quickly master them and then practice them in ongoing PBL units. Therefore, these are most appropriately considered student-directed learning skills, since they help students organize and direct their own learning in PBL tasks. Further, much less instruction in these skills is necessary over time, as students become more adept in these skills.

Brainstorming and Group Processing

When an anchor and driving question is developed at the beginning of a PBL unit, the first group process most classes engage in involves brainstorming on that driving question in order to generate ideas about how the PBL group may wish to initiate and complete that task (Barell, 2007; Grant, 2010). As students become more adept in PBL learning environments, teachers may allow and encourage them to develop assignments or artifacts during the brainstorming process, though initially teachers are likely to develop these assignments in some rudimentary form and then offer students choices about which assignments their group would like to complete. In essence, brainstorming represents a group's ability to collectively think through a PBL task, exploring the ramifications of it and generating a list of possible topics or activities that might be undertaken in completion of the PBL work. As such, brainstorming skills are critical in PBL instruction (Grant, 2010).

When instruction migrates toward increased use of PBL instructional formats—instructional procedures that tend to be much more dependent on successful group functioning—most teachers find that it is advisable to directly teach brainstorming skills to their class initially (Grant, 2010). This is because brainstorming, as practiced in PBL projects, involves much more than merely idea generation. At a minimum, brainstorming involves the entire skill set presented in Box 5.1.

Box 5.1 Brainstorming Skills

- Identify, consider, and stick to a broad topic without ranging too far afield.
- Generate ideas that differ from those previously presented.
- List all ideas without any initial editing or elimination of the concepts.
- Encourage others to think independently and differently about the topic.
- Focus on generation of as many ideas as possible without losing the broad topic.
- Refuse to limit the idea or concept list, even if a glaring logical gap or flaw in an idea is obvious.
- Respect all ideas as worthy of some consideration.
- Hold a closing phase in which ideas are compared and synthesized (i.e., placing two ideas together if they represent the same broader idea and if the persons suggesting those ideas agree to place them together as one idea).
- Demonstrate encouragement and respect for all discussion participants.

As this skills list indicates, brainstorming includes teaching respect for the ideas of others, peer encouragement, and other group process skills that would be of benefit to many students in schools today regardless of the task at hand. Again, while undue time should not be spent teaching brainstorming during every PBL unit, some time on brainstorming, at least initially, will benefit the class and enhance the initial PBL experience. Generating a poster of these brainstorming skills (and others that the teacher may wish to emphasize), and discussing that with the class, or perhaps presenting these as the "Rules of Brainstorming!" is well advised. By leaving that poster visible throughout the year, teachers can refer back to it if and when behavior problems erupt among students. A few additional guidelines for teaching brainstorming skills are presented in Box 5.2.

Box 5.2 Teaching Brainstorming Skills

1. Develop a poster that summarizes the brainstorming skills you wish to emphasize (using example indicators from Box 5.1 in this chapter).

2. Prior to the initial brainstorming session, the teacher should appoint two persons from within the group to serve as the recorder of ideas and the discussion leader. The teacher should then explain their roles to them.

3. During the initial instruction (i.e., the first brainstorming session), the teacher should review the guidelines on the poster and then lead the brainstorming discussion.

4. Assign the recorder of ideas to go to the dry-erase board or interactive whiteboard. Their task will be to write a brief synopsis of each idea or thought presented.

5. The discussion leader's task will be to make certain everyone's idea is given a hearing and to attempt to involve all participants in suggesting ideas.

6. The discussion leader should guard against anyone's idea being interrupted or criticized during the initial brainstorming.

7. Hold a brainstorming session with the recorder and discussion leader moderating the session. The teacher

(Continued)

Box 5.2 (Continued)

should step in only if necessary to help moderate the brainstorming session.

8. At some point, the discussion leader should suggest ideas that might be "merged" or that seem to state the same general idea. The discussion leader should state why he or she recommends synthesis of those ideas and then request permission to merge them from participants that suggested the ideas originally.

9. After the synthesis phase is complete, have the recorder write down all synthesized ideas and all remaining ideas from the board, make copies, and hand those to all participants.

10. In future brainstorming sessions, the students should select their own recorder and discussion leader, and the discussion leader should review the rules of brainstorming on the poster prior to each session.

Time Line Planning

Students embarking on a PBL project will also be involved in planning instructional activities within a given time frame during the specified PBL unit, and that will require some knowledge of how to "time line" out the various artifacts required within a project. While time lines vary considerably from project to project, some givens in the overall time line requirements are typically presented in the original PBL project description. For example, in the PBL project on planning a Civil War memorial garden (described in Box 4.9 in Chapter 4), a total of 15 separate assignments or artifacts were required, and six of those assignments stated a given due date for that specific assignment.

> Students embarking on a PBL project will also be involved in planning instructional activities within a given time frame during the specified PBL unit, and that will require some knowledge of how to "time line" out the various artifacts required within a project.

In helping students learn the skill of time line planning, teachers may wish to use a time line template such as that presented in Box 5.3. Of course, this template may be adapted as necessary to address the number and types of required assignments or artifacts.

Box 5.3 Sample Class Time Line for the Civil War Memorial Garden Project

This project requires completion of the following assignments and development of the following artifacts. Beside each, the PBL group should assign a definitive due date, and for those assignments and artifacts that are more complex (indicated with an asterisk), the PBL group should also list a "draft assignment due date."

1. Four webquests:

    Causes of the Civil War _____
    Presidents from 1820 to 1877 _____
    Critical battles of the war _____
    Westward expansion and slavery _____

2. Jigsaw on North Carolina battles _____

3. Weekly class wiki entries (check off for each student each week) _____

4. Weekly student journal entries (check off for each student each week) _____

5. Biography of important person* draft date _____

    Final biography date _____

6. Completion of Flight to Freedom game (by end of Week 3; list students in PBL group as they complete this assignment) _____

7. Creative Products*: List each product and date completed. Must be completed by Week 6 of the project. Draft due date _____

    Final project due date _____

8. Planning time line (within Week 1) _____

9. Planning assignments by students (within Week 1) _____

    _____

10. Diagram (due two weeks prior to project end)

    _____

11. The Battlefield Commission presentation (due by Wednesday of Week 9) _____

    _____

Sample Class Time Line for the Civil War Memorial Garden Project

There is an additional advantage to teaching about time line development. While time lines have been presented in the discussion earlier as organizational planning tools for students to use when mapping out a PBL project, time lines in some cases might also be very effective project artifact assignments within a PBL project. For example, in a high school biology class investigating bacteria, a time line of the discovery of bacteria through the development of antibacterial medicines might be an excellent artifact to require within the PBL project. Of course, social studies and history offer many opportunities to teach via time lines that students develop, since so much of that curriculum is tied to temporal units of study. However, many examples in virtually any subject area can involve developing time lines as either educational planning tools or project artifacts themselves. In general, teachers should seek ways to have students develop time lines in various PBL projects, as this skill also transfers quite readily to the working world of the 21st century.

In fact, Larmer et al. (2009) coupled the time line planning emphasis with the concept of group management of a PBL project. This idea incorporates both the time line planning required and some of the management questions involved with a PBL project. Thus, this type of project management tool includes information beyond the time line such as due dates for draft artifacts or products, whose responsibility it is to develop those, and who evaluates those products for the group. A sample tool for project management is presented in Box 5.4.

Other Metacognitive Planning Tools

In addition to brainstorming and time line planning skills, students in lower and middle grade levels can benefit greatly by learning other metacognitive planning skills. Because of the expectation within PBL that students undertake responsibility for planning many of the instructional activities, mastery of some common instructional planning tools is very useful, and various metacognitive tools can be of use in helping students understand the planning process, as well as the instructional content.

Metacognitive planning tools assist students in thinking about their own level of understanding of the content and monitoring their own progress toward the overall PBL goal. While such tools do not themselves represent conceptual material to be learned, the use of various metacognitive tools can greatly facilitate student-directed inquiry, either for an individual student or for the PBL group as a whole.

Box 5.4 Project Management Responsibilities Schedule

Group Artifacts or Assignments	Draft Date	Final Date	Who Evaluates This

Individual Assignments	Who Does This	Draft Date	Final Date	Who Evaluates This

Teachers have used metacognitive tools in the classroom for many years, and while most students in the middle elementary grades have been exposed to these tools, students may not have been challenged to develop these tools themselves for specific tasks or to decide whether or not to use these tools in a given situation. Students may lack the ability to select specific tools for specific types of group-task planning. Thus, PBL teachers may be called upon to teach about the common metacognitive planning tools and instruct students in their use (Barell, 2007). Here are a few examples that have been recommended within the context of PBL instruction.

KWL charts: As one commonly used metacognitive tool, teachers in a PBL unit might share the idea of using a simple KWL chart with their students (Barell, 2007; Baron, 2011). The KWL chart, originally developed by Ogle (1986), focuses on three questions that help students understand where they are in relation to specific content:

K   *Know*   (What do I know about this presently?)

W   *Want to Know* (What do I want to know or understand?)

L   *Learned*   (What have I learned in this process?)

This KWL method involves putting a blank KWL chart before an individual or a group of students and having them discuss the first two questions prior to reading a short text selection. By identifying what students already know about a topic, the PBL group will be activating prior knowledge. Also, having students identify what they might want to know in the second question invites students to exercise some choice relative to the assignment regarding what they might wish to study. Students would then address the last question (What have I learned?) after they have read and discussed a text on their general topic.

Of course, variations of this chart have been proposed that allow students to use this in longer-term assignments, such as brainstorming the PBL work at the beginning of a project, or using this as a prelude to a minilesson within the project itself. Box 5.5 presents a KWN chart, a modification of the KWL chart, that might be used in a longer assignment within a PBL unit. Note that the last question has been modified a bit (What do I *need* to learn?) in order to allow for the fact that not all of the desired information might be mastered during a quick reading of only one short passage. Thus, a KWN chart can be used as a preliminary tool that students revisit throughout a longer time frame. Finally, this KWN chart includes several spaces for notes on interesting points at the bottom, since, the more complex the topic is, the more likely that some factual items or points might not fit easily within the three question areas at the top. In PBL, teachers and students should feel free to adapt this KWL chart idea in any way they like that suits the needs of the PBL group.

Box 5.5 A KWN Chart for a PBL Unit

Know What do I know?	**Want** What do I want to know?	**Need** What do I need to know?

Other Important Points:

Concept maps: Concept maps, sometimes referred to as semantic maps or semantic webs, present concepts in relation to each other in some type of meaningful pictorial form, and various proponents of PBL have recommended the use of concept mapping during PBL instruction to emphasize higher-order thinking skills (Barell, 2007; Schlemmer & Schlemmer, 2008). Development of a concept map can assist students in nurturing a deeper understanding of content as well as provide a tool to assist them in remembering content, since pictorial representations of information typically are associated with higher levels of retention. A concept map that might be used in the Civil War memorial garden project described in Chapter 4 is presented in Box 5.6.

Note that this concept map does not attempt to present all of the content covered within the project, but rather, it focuses on a significant aspect of that unit—potential causes of the conflict as they relate to the changing sensitivities of various groups that were historically impacted by the Civil War. A concept map of this nature can help teach the relationships between one's perspective and one's understanding of the sensitive history of this period.

Box 5.6 Concept Map on the Civil War Memorial Garden Project

| Groups Historically Impacted by the War | Potential Causes of the Civil War | | |
	Slavery	*Sectional or Economic Differences (North vs. South)*	*Federal Interference in State Governance*
Descendants of Those Enslaved			
Descendants of Confederate Soldiers			
Descendants of Union Soldiers			
General Public in North Carolina			
General Public			

Student Creativity Within PBL Projects

As discussed in Chapter 4, many proponents of technology or PBL in the classroom suggest that the very meaning of teaching and learning is changing and that students are becoming creative agents in the learning process during the 21st century (Bender & Waller, 2011; Boss & Krauss, 2007; Ferriter & Garry, 2010). In the context of the 21st-century classroom, teaching is transformed into facilitating learning rather than leading learning, and learning changes into creation of content rather than passive consumption of content. In the classrooms of tomorrow, content is created by students, content that is newly synthesized in novel ways to address specific, authentic, and highly meaningful problems. Thus, student-directed inquiry in the context of PBL should emphasize instruction that helps students generate high-quality content and then present that content in order to display deep understanding of the issues and topics discussed.

Chapter 4 mentioned the use of digital cameras in a variety of PBL projects, and the Civil War memorial garden project described in that same chapter involved a culminating assignment that was technology based—a PowerPoint presentation, including digital video examples, for the final PBL project. As these examples illustrate, the student-directed inquiry nature of PBL projects frequently results in actual synthesis of information in digital form that addresses a specific problem or driving question. Unlike the passive learning that characterized the traditional classrooms of yesteryear, students in PBL classrooms are creators of knowledge (Boss & Krauss, 2007; Larmer et al., 2009; Partnership for 21st Century Skills, 2009; Schlemmer & Schlemmer, 2008).

While such knowledge creation most often involves innovative use of modern technologies, that is not always the case. For example, traditional assignments such as book reports, creative themes, and position papers might be one artifact within a PBL project, and an increasing emphasis on PBL should not mean the wholesale abandonment of assignments of this type that many students have found meaningful. This section describes a variety of end products that might evolve from either technology-based on nontechnology-based PBL work.

> The increasing emphasis on PBL should not mean the wholesale abandonment of assignment formats that many students have found meaningful.

Podcast Development

One technology creation option within a PBL framework involves student generation of a podcast (Salend, 2009). Podcasts are digital media files that might present information in the form of a radio talk show. While the term *podcast* originally referred to audio files, today, both audio and digital video files are considered podcasts. Podcasts are typically fairly brief (e.g., two to five minutes) and include information on a highly specific topic. These files can be found on the Internet in many locations and can typically be downloaded to individual classroom computers or, in some cases, to personal audio devices such as an MP3 player or iPod.

Because students love using these newer technologies, teachers have found many creative ways to download and use podcasts, and the excitement generated by podcasts truly motivates students to work harder to understand the topic more completely (Salend, 2009). Further, having students develop podcasts as artifacts within a PBL assignment motivates them, since any podcast may be uploaded to the school website, or the Internet, as discussed in Chapter 3. The creative assignment in the Civil War memorial garden project described in Chapter 4 provided an assignment option for the creation of a video project, and virtually all recent PBL examples emphasize this technology-based option.

> Podcasts are digital audio or video files that represent informational "episodes" addressing a particular content topic and typically can be created by students and subsequently downloaded onto a computer.

Like many other skills described in this section, teachers will initially need to teach students how to develop an appropriate and effective podcast. However, this task is not as daunting as it may sound, since, in many ways, development of either an audio or a video podcast is similar to developing a comprehensive written theme, position paper, or term paper, and that similarity should certainly be noted when teaching students how to develop a podcast.

The guidelines presented in Box 5.7 will assist in this instruction. Further, these general organizational skills are highly similar to the preparation steps in developing a PowerPoint presentation or any other type of evidence presentation. Finally, as shown in these guidelines for the generation of podcast content, students in this process will also learn skills related to evaluation of evidence, presenting an effective argument, and interpreting information from the Internet or other sources. These are and will continue to be critical skills in the information-overload world of the 21st century.

Box 5.7 Developing an Effective Podcast

1. Select a broad theme related to the topic to be covered. This may or may not involve the entire content of a longer PBL project, so the group may wish to set some parameters on what is to be included and what is not.

2. List the main ideas within that topic and organize them in some specific order (either temporal, or cause and effect, or related ideas). Each of those main ideas will probably become a segment of content within the podcast.

3. Once the main ideas are listed and organized, find factual information related to each. In this context, look for the factual evidence and points or ideas that the group wishes to put forth related to each main idea.

4. On a piece of paper, or using computer software, the group should organize the main ideas and supporting points and evidence in outline form.

5. Next, using the outline, the group should develop a storyboard. With the outline as a basis, the group should consider what pictorial or audio evidence might be found to support the points in the outline. Then, place segments of the outline on a large piece of poster paper in sequence order and draw or list video or audio examples under each.

6. Next, seek select video and/or audio content that supports those broad ideas or the points related to them. Visual evidence supporting one's perspective is always desirable and can help the group "make the case."

7. Demonstrate a willingness to be critical of the evidence that supports your perspective, since such a critical stance tends to help you advocate for your ideas with your audience. Discuss the quality of the evidence (expert opinion, hard research evidence, opinion of uninvolved persons, unsupported opinions or allegations, etc.) and be willing to amend or change your perspective as you evaluate the evidence.

8. Include within your storyboard evidence that does not support your point. You should present contrary evidence since integrity demands a full presentation, and your

(Continued)

Box 5.7 (Continued)

audience will discount your overall perspective if all reasonable evidence and ideas are not given some attention.

9. You may opt to deflate the importance of evidence that argues against your main points in two ways: (a) critique the quality of the evidence in some fashion or (b) use a "weight of the evidence" stance, suggesting that while some evidence is contrary, most of the evidence supports your point.

10. Put the pieces together and edit to make them seamlessly fit into a video or audio podcast lasting from two to five minutes.

Other Creative Assignment Options for Students Within PBL

While student creation of podcasts has been widely discussed in the educational literature (Cote, 2007; Salend, 2009), other products likewise offer creation options for students. For example, students in some PBL projects have developed puzzles or games that might be used to teach specific content. The creation of a simple crossword puzzle using vocabulary from a PBL unit can greatly enhance instruction, and while some students may receive credit for this artifact when they develop the crossword puzzle in a PBL project, other students might subsequently use this puzzle simply as a learning tool within a PBL unit. Development of various board games can also present opportunities for students to creatively develop something that assists in learning content.

The creation of various ARGs might likewise provide a creative option for students to demonstrate their learning. In the alternative reality game Second Life (www.secondlife.com; discussed in Chapter 4), any player is offered the opportunity to create a "destination" that may be fantasy based, whimsical, or historically based. For example, within Second Life, several destinations are presented that deal with the study of pirates, and these could be used as a teaching tool within a history unit on that topic. Alternatively, students might be challenged to create another pirate world reflective of the life of a favorite pirate or pirates associated with the history of a given area.

Of course, many teachers have provided nontechnology-based creative writing opportunities for students throughout the years in a wide variety of curricular areas. Students with a strength in literacy or linguistic skills might benefit from creative writing projects as they develop an artifact for the PBL project. These may range from one-act plays, to poetry, to short-story writing that demonstrates knowledge within a specific area. Again, teachers have used these types of creative production assignments for many years, and these types of assignments do fit nicely within the PBL framework. Certainly such assignment options should be included within virtually every PBL project in some form in order to stress creativity and creative thinking throughout the school curriculum.

Teacher-Directed Strategies in PBL

Grouping Students for PBL Instruction

Because PBL strongly emphasizes social learning, much of the work in PBL is done in groups (Barell, 2010; Boss & Krauss, 2007; Larmer et al., 2009), and various authors recommend different group sizes. Larmer et al. (2009) recommend four students as a workable group size for PBL projects, while others have discussed groups that range in size from eight to twelve (Barell, 2010; Bender & Crane, 2011). Of course, these recommendations will result in different numbers of PBL groups within the class, and more PBL groups results in more monitoring of different group projects for the teacher. Still, teachers monitor group work all the time in their classes, and that will not be an undue burden in the PBL framework. Also, teachers should have the flexibility to use larger groups for some PBL projects and smaller groups for other projects.

However, not all grouping considerations involve size. Schlemmer and Schlemmer (2008) described a variety of grouping options, with the groups based on ability levels of the students in the group, student interests, or group learning styles. In some PBL projects it may be advantageous to form groups that involve students from different PBL groups for various minilessons or specific tasks.

Finally, teachers should realize that not all tasks within a given PBL project will involve group work or cooperative work. For example, participation in a class wiki might be considered as an individual assignment for each student, while other work might involve having students work together in pairs. At other times, students will be collaborating with their PBL group or possibly with the class as a whole during minilessons on a given topic.

Individual Work Within PBL

There are many opportunities within a PBL framework for students to engage in individual projects. For example, for artistically talented students working within a PBL project, the creation of paintings, drawings, or sculpted art projects as artifacts that demonstrate knowledge and relate to the broader PBL project is sometimes necessary. Certainly PBL offers the opportunity to differentiate the lessons based on individual talents of the students within a PBL group, and teachers should use differentiated assignments within PBL to increase students' motivation to participate in the PBL project.

> PBL offers the opportunity to differentiate the lessons based on individual talents of the students within a PBL group, and teachers should use differentiated assignments within PBL to increase students' motivation to participate in the PBL project.

For example, virtually every veteran teacher has worked with artistically talented students who likewise demonstrate low motivation to participate in group work. In planning differentiated instructional activities within a PBL assignment, those students should be provided an opportunity to use their artistic talents in individual work that provides an artifact for the PBL group as a whole. Other students may be skilled or highly motivated to participate in class activities when music is involved. These students may work individually developing lyrics on the PBL project topic that "fit" with their favorite rhythm, a popular tune, or music genre. For example, a "country music sounding" summary of major points on a topic or a hip-hop rhythm summation of the same information might be developed by students in the PBL project. Offering students the choice of musical genres to use can motivate the students to participate in that activity and will typically result in a better product. Once a "content rich" rhythm or tune is developed, it can be videotaped as one artifact for the PBL project as a whole.

Partner Work Within PBL

Like the individual work just described, PBL provides many opportunities for peer buddies or partner work within the context of a broader PBL project. The tried and true Think-Pair-Share tactic (Adams & Hamm, 1994; Johnson & Johnson, 1999; Johnson, Johnson, & Smith, 1991, 2007) fits nicely within the PBL framework. Think-Pair-Share is a cooperative learning strategy that incorporates individuals, partners, and sharing of the partner work with the larger group (Schlemmer & Schlemmer, 2008). To use the strategy, teachers pose a particular question or problem to the class as a whole. Each student is required to think individually for a specified amount of time to formulate a personal opinion or solution. Students are then put into pairs where they share with each other their own answers to the posed problem. This partner pairing step provides opportunity for students to articulate their ideas and listen to the ideas of others. This step allows time for students to jointly construct meaning from the content as well as reflect on their own understanding and ultimately synthesize their concepts with information from their peers. Further, this step in the process can provide fodder for students to consider reflectively in their journals within a PBL project.

Finally, the pairs are called upon to share their findings with the larger PBL group or perhaps with the entire class. In order to prepare for this broader presentation, some teachers provide a template, such as the one provided in Box 5.8, to help students record their thoughts during the partner activity. This type of template will help students process their own thoughts while working with their peer partner, as well as ensure accountability for completion of the Think-Pair-Share activity and provide documentation of student effort for the teacher.

Box 5.8 A Think-Pair-Share Template

Think

Review the information you have on this topic and then list several ideas you have about the topic. Write enough down to help you remember the whole idea.

1. _____

2. _____

3. _____

(Continued)

Box 5.8 (Continued)

Pair

Talk with your partner and explain each of your ideas. Then have your partner explain his or her ideas to you. While you talk, record any new ideas that you discover together.

1. _____

2. _____

3. _____

Share

Looking at all of these ideas, you and your partner have to decide which idea or ideas are most important. You can share one or two ideas with the whole group (but no more!). List these ideas here that you intend to share.

1. _____

2. _____

Cooperative Learning Strategies Within PBL

Once students are placed within their groups for the PBL learning experience, they will be working collaboratively on a wide array of tasks. While PBL instruction includes some work that can be done individually or with partners (e.g., webquests, participation in wikis, library or text research, etc.), much of the work of PBL involves collaborative problem solving with groups of other students. Thus, students in PBL are expected to learn in a collaborative, cooperative fashion, as well as independently (Johnson & Johnson, 2010; Johnson et al., 2007; Tsay & Brady, 2010).

Like PBL, cooperative learning is built upon the idea that students learn most effectively through social contexts and interaction with their peers to build each other's conceptual understanding (Adams & Hamm, 1994; Johnson et al., 2007; Tsay & Brady, 2010). This is one advantage of cooperative instruction that probably results in higher levels of student engagement. Specifically, teachers have long recognized that students frequently pay more attention to other students in the class than to teachers, and cooperative learning, like PBL, takes advantage of this fact (Adams & Hamm, 1994; Johnson & Johnson, 2010; Tsay & Brady, 2010).

> Like PBL instruction, cooperative learning practices are precipitated on students working together to build each other's conceptual understanding.

While many teachers today use cooperative learning assignments in a stand-alone manner, cooperative instruction is also an integral part of project-based learning projects. In fact, various cooperative learning assignments may be implemented as minilessons within a longer-term PBL project. Also, these cooperative learning assignments may allow teachers to differentiate instruction by having some struggling students complete these assignments to shore up their understanding of the content, whereas more advanced students may skip some of the cooperative assignments in a PBL instructional unit in order to spend more time on other project assignments and artifacts. Of course, unlike PBL projects in general, many cooperative learning assignments can easily be completed in a single instructional period (Johnson & Johnson, 2010; Johnson et al., 2007; Tsay & Brady, 2010). Other cooperative learning assignments may be spread over two or more days.

Teaching Cooperative Learning Skills

Teachers moving toward PBL instruction should understand that students will need cooperative learning skills for the PBL instruction to be effective. It is not appropriate to merely place students in cooperative groups for PBL and assume that those students know how to effectively work together in a problem-solving context. Successful cooperative learning is more structured than the occasional group project type of task in a traditional classroom, and beyond brainstorming, cooperative learning should include skills such as group processing, individual and group accountability, and interpersonal skills (Johnson & Johnson, 2010; Johnson et al., 2007; Tsay & Brady, 2010). Teachers might need to take some extra time with some students to teach conflict management strategies, decision-making strategies, or effective personal communication skills (Johnson & Johnson, 2010; Tsay & Brady, 2010) in order to make cooperative learning experiences successful for all class members.

Also, in order for cooperative learning groups to work, sufficient time must be provided for students to work together allowing for questions, challenges, critiques, and suggestions (Tsay & Brady, 2010). Although there may be need for students to work individually on the projects at some point, there must also be ample face-to-face interaction among group members. This provides opportunity for students to learn from each other, ask questions about content and strategy, and carefully monitor group progress.

Finally, cooperative learning provides the teacher with an opportunity to stress group interdependence in PBL instruction. Each member of a cooperative learning group should be encouraged to understand that the success or failure of the group depends on contributions of every member and that all of the group must deal with the consequences if one member does not participate (Johnson & Johnson, 2010). With that noted, both individual and group accountability should be stressed in cooperative learning tasks, and the smaller the group, the more responsible for the end product each group member is likely to feel.

A Jigsaw Within a PBL Project

As the discussion earlier indicates, PBL projects are greatly facilitated when all participating students have good cooperative learning skills. While all classes (as well as all individual students) will probably demonstrate different learning curves on these skills as they move toward mastery, teachers implementing PBL are well advised to begin by teaching cooperative learning skills by embedding them within more traditional instructional units first. The goal is to teach these important interaction skills to the students prior to jumping into a full-fledged PBL unit. Teachers might well begin this cooperative instruction with a simple jigsaw activity.

The jigsaw tactic was one of the early cooperative learning approaches described in the literature (Adams & Hamm, 1994; Johnson et al., 2007), and PBL advocates have recommended this tactic specifically for PBL instruction (Schlemmer & Schlemmer, 2008). In this cooperative learning strategy, groups of students are formed, but only part of the subject area content is provided to participants in each group. Therefore, group members in a jigsaw group are viewed as "experts" on their particular topic, but they must ultimately fit their information together (like a jigsaw puzzle) in order to help each student in the group grasp the entire concept. In this approach, each group member is dependent on every other member in the jigsaw group for some of the necessary content.

Using the PBL project on the Civil War memorial garden described in Box 4.9 in Chapter 4 as an example, a cooperative learning jigsaw task might be created to teach specific content within that broader project. For example, that PBL instructional unit would probably include some content on important Civil War battles in North Carolina. A teacher could use the jigsaw to teach that content during a multiday activity within that PBL unit. In most cases, between four and six groups within the class works nicely for this type of jigsaw activity, and those jigsaw groups may be created from within the PBL group or within the class as a whole.

In order to begin the jigsaw, members from each jigsaw group would either choose or be assigned specific content to study about, in this case, individual Civil War battles in North Carolina. First, students might brainstorm as a whole-class activity on the various Civil War battles in North Carolina and discuss the relative importance of each. Then, students could form the different jigsaw groups. Within each group, students would be assigned a particular battle to study, and thus each student becomes an "expert" on that battle. Expert teams would then be formed including experts from across the jigsaw groups that are studying the same battle. One expert team might study the battle of Fort Fisher in Wilmington that closed the final blockader port in the entire Confederacy. Another expert team might study the first battle of New Bern that won the Carolina coast for the Union.

Once each expert team gathered all of their information and discussed that information together in some fashion, the original jigsaw groups would be reformed. At that point, each expert within the jigsaw group would present their information to the rest of the jigsaw team, thus patching all of that information together in a jigsaw.

The cooperative learning jigsaw team would then use the information from each expert to put together a complete presentation on the important Civil War battles in North Carolina. A sample jigsaw lesson plan is presented for a seventh-grade classroom in Box 5.9. This jigsaw example could easily fit within the PBL project described in Chapter 4, and we should highlight the active nature of this learning procedure. In this example, students would be mastering content in a jigsaw fashion rather than passively receiving information from the teacher.

Box 5.9 Jigsaw Sample Lesson Plan

Seventh-Grade North Carolina History Standard

Describe the critical Civil War battles in North Carolina that impacted the state as well as the overall outcome of the Civil War as a whole.

Note: This standard provides the content that is intended to be covered in this jigsaw example. While the list of battles that follows would need to be covered, students would be expected to determine why these are critically important in the broader Civil War history. Thus, the sentences relative to the importance of each battle are provided here only for clarification purposes, and those points would not be provided initially to students.

The Battle of New Bern (March 14, 1862). Union captured a port city in North Carolina, stationed 16,000 troops there, and used that as a point of control for actions throughout Eastern Carolina through the end of the war.

The Battle of Fort Macon (March 21, 1862). The Union bombarded Fort Macon and thereby captured the port of Beaufort/Morehead City, from which they staged the Union blockade of all ports along the Atlantic seaboard from the Chesapeake Bay in Virginia down through Southern Florida.

The Battle of Plymouth (April 19, 1864). Confederates recapture a Union-held port city on the Albemarle Sound using a new weapon, a Confederate ironclad—the *Ram Albemarle*. Within two months, the *Albemarle* sinks four Union blockade ships, threatens to reduce the Union blockade of coastal ports, and is seen in the Union as a potential threat on the Union capital in Washington, DC, since the ironclad ram seemed unsinkable. However, the *Ram Albemarle* was sunk in Plymouth by a daring Union commando raid that boarded the ship and sunk her at the dock of Plymouth.

The Battle of Fort Fisher (Jan. 17, 1865). The Union captured this fort and closed the port of Wilmington 20 miles upriver to blockade runners. Wilmington was the last open Confederate port, so this battle directly led to the end of the war only three months later.

Battle of Bentonville (March 17–19, 1865). Last large-scale battle of the Civil War, with 60,000 Union forces under

(Continued)

Box 5.9 (Continued)

General Sherman defeating 39,000 Confederates under General Joe Johnson. Led to the surrender of Johnson's army only a month later, some two weeks after General Robert E. Lee's surrender in Virginia.

Jigsaw Procedures

1. Within a PBL project, students have been provided with information from their text on the Civil War in North Carolina, as well as various Internet sources on battles within the state. Initially, within a whole-class brainstorming minilesson, students must discuss and determine the importance of various North Carolina Civil War battles. The students select the battles based on these discussions.

2. Five different jigsaw groups, each of which will include five students, will be formed. Each student within each group will be assigned one particular battle on which that student will become an "expert."

3. The "expert groups" meet to study and discuss their assigned battle. This will be accomplished in three 20-minute sessions at the first of each history period on three consecutive days. In the first two 20-minute periods, students will research the battle and individually identify critical points about the battle for later discussion. Students may use the text, Internet resources, and media center resources to investigate these battles.

4. On the last 20-minute period, each student presents the critical points he or she notes, and then the group jointly determines which points should be taught to the whole class. At the end of this period, each expert group should have a "final copy" paragraph or set of points that must be taught to all class members relative to their particular battle. At that point, the expert groups disband.

5. On the next two days, students will work in their jigsaw groups, teaching each other about the critical information about each battle. Thus, information on all of these critically important battles is provided to all students in the class by the end of the last 20-minute jigsaw period.

Advantages of Cooperative Learning

Cooperative learning approaches like the jigsaw have been shown to be effective instructional approaches (Johnson et al., 2007; Marzano et al., 2001; Tsay & Brady, 2010; Wachanga & Mwangi, 2004). Because cooperative learning encourages students to take a hands-on, highly active approach to learning, research has shown academic improvement gains as high as 28 percent for students within cooperative learning groups (Marzano et al., 2001).

> Research has shown academic improvement gains as high as 28 percent for students within cooperative learning groups.

In cooperative learning groups, students become familiar with the new content and also learn critical 21st-century group-work skills by working with peers of varying backgrounds, academic levels, and cultural attitudes. Students in this instructional paradigm learn to interact successfully with others as they construct and synthesize information to explain new concepts and develop solutions to problems (Adams & Hamm, 1994; Tsay & Brady, 2010). Cooperative learning activities force students to synthesize their own information with information from their peers while evaluating the information as a whole (Tsay & Brady, 2010). Thus, students learn to listen to views of others and participate effectively in group work, and this results in demonstrative academic gains associated with cooperative learning instruction (Johnson et al., 2007; Tsay & Brady, 2010; Wachanga & Mwangi, 2004). Of course, many of these advantages of cooperative learning parallel the goals of PBL instruction as a whole, so the cooperative learning approach, while it has been around for a long while, fits nicely within the emerging PBL instructional paradigm.

Scaffolded Instruction Within PBL

Teacher-led minilessons, as one component of PBL, were described in Chapter 3 of this text, and such minilessons can include virtually any teaching technique used in more traditional classes. However, one teaching strategy that fits particularly well as a minilesson within the PBL framework is scaffolding. Scaffolding is a way of framing instruction on new topics with instructional supports while simultaneously relating the new content to previously taught content in order to build deeper conceptual understandings (Cole & Wahsburn-Moses, 2010).

In particular, when some students demonstrate limited understanding of some of the content, the teacher might choose to undertake a scaffolded minilesson by pulling those students aside for scaffolded instruction on that particular topic. In many cases, struggling students need to be shown a specific concept as it relates to previously mastered material, and scaffoled instruction is one way to do that. The mechanism of learning support that is used to bridge those two concepts is the scaffold, and it may involve teacher think-alouds, teacher modeling of the problem, a hard-copy concept map, or a set of instructions on how to complete a particular math operation such as addition of two-digit numbers with regrouping, as related to two-digit addition without regrouping.

Scaffolds are not intended as permanent supports for the student but rather as "bridging" mechanisms that help a student move from his or her present level of understanding to a new and deeper conceptual understanding of the content (Cole & Wahsburn-Moses, 2010; Schlemmer & Schlemmer, 2008). Therefore, if a hard-copy item such as a list of "Steps in this type of problem" checklist is used initially, it should be withdrawn as a support or scaffold for the student after the student has internalized those steps.

> Scaffolding is a way of framing instruction on new topics with instructional supports while simultaneously relating the new content to previously taught content in order to build deeper conceptual understandings.

Both scaffolding and PBL in general share a common goal in terms of seeking to build deeper conceptual understanding on the part of the students, and both tend to emphasize active student involvement within the lesson activities. Therefore, fitting scaffolded lessons into a PBL unit as minilessons on a small segment of the content is very appropriate, and teachers will probably find themselves doing a series of scaffolded minilessons within a PBL unit. In fact, proponents of PBL have specifically recommended scaffolded instruction as an important instructional component within the PBL framework (Bender & Crane, 2011; Schlemmer & Schlemmer, 2008).

Showing those mental connections between concepts can easily be built into a 10- or 15-minute scaffolded minilesson. Thus, by working with a few struggling students as other students in the class work on other assignments within the PBL unit, the teacher can assist students who are having difficulty with newer or more complex material. Often, after very little instructional time in the scaffolded minilesson, the correct mental connections are made, and the struggling student has one of those "aha!" learning moments in which he or she grasps the concept for the first time. Therefore, teachers should certainly develop scaffolded minilesson options with most PBL projects.

Classroom Control: Preplanned Activities or Teaching on the Fly?

Given this array of technological instructional approaches, as discussed in Chapter 4, and the nontechnological instructional approaches presented here, some teachers may wonder how similar the planning for PBL instruction and more traditional instructional units might be. Of course, not all instructional ideas presented in this book on PBL (or in any other book) will be implemented in every PBL unit, and most will probably not be included in a teacher's first PBL instructional unit unless that teacher is already familiar with these teaching ideas. Still, teachers must be assured that PBL teaching is still teaching, and thus, veteran teachers can move into PBL with confidence that their instructional skills—teaching skills that have been honed and refined over many years in the classroom—will still be very much relevant for teaching within the PBL instructional paradigm. While other skills (e.g., upgraded technology skills, etc.) may also become necessary, teachers will generally develop those skills as they move forward within the PBL instructional framework. Again, as recommended previously, all teachers should begin PBL instruction now, starting with a subject and teaching ideas that place them within their comfort zone and move from there into newer instructional techniques.

> Veteran teachers can move into PBL with confidence that their instructional skills will still be very much relevant for teaching within the PBL instructional paradigm.

Still, the issue of classroom control is critical when teachers begin to move toward PBL instruction. When presented with these instructional options, and with the idea that students' decisions will be driving much of the instruction in PBL, most teachers do wonder about overall "control" of their classroom. One hears questions like this:

- Will PBL planning be similar to planning more traditional instructional units or will I be teaching on the fly?
- How can I prepare for PBL?
- Will I know what is going to take place in the classroom on any given day?

On these questions, teachers should put their minds at ease. As described in Chapter 3, PBL instruction and planning is very much a front-loaded planning endeavor for the teacher. Given this array of instructional options, teachers new to PBL can easily devise an initial long-term PBL project over a four-, six-, or nine-week time frame and feel comfortable that their class will function effectively. In that context, teachers may initially identify the overall PBL project, and perhaps a couple of driving questions, and then guide students in selecting one of them. Teachers will then carefully map out the related Common Core State Standards to be covered. Next, teachers will develop a project outline such as the one shown in Box 4.9, and that project outline will present an array of project assignments, artifacts, or assignment options for students to complete.

Larmer et al. (2009) urge teachers to plan PBL units with the end product or products in mind. In that sense, once a broad project idea is identified and content standards are considered, teachers should move to some type of description of the end product, products, and artifacts that will show mastery of the content. Finally, in that context, teachers may then select the specific instructional strategies they wish to employ, from the range of instructional options presented in this chapter and in Chapter 4. Thus, before the PBL project begins, teachers have some grasp of the instructional strategies they intend to use at various points within the classroom, and at the beginning of each class period, teachers will have a firm understanding of what is to take place within and among the various PBL groups. In fact, at no point during a PBL project should the teacher begin a period without a firm idea of what is to take place within each PBL group in the classroom (Barell, 2007, 2010; Boss & Krauss, 2007; Larmer et al., 2009).

With that noted, because students are taking more initiative in developing instructional activities, flexibility is one key to successful PBL instruction (Barell, 2007; Boss & Krauss, 2007). PBL instruction must include some flexible options within the schedule. As every veteran teacher realizes, there will still be occasions within a four-, nine-, or sixteen-week project in which the teacher must offer an unplanned minilesson to some students or where a single PBL group needs one more day to complete a jigsaw activity, an art project, or an artifact within a PBL project. Thus, some flexibility in the PBL schedule is necessary during virtually all projects. Further, teachers and students alike must use effective time line planning as described previously to assure that most of the scheduled work is completed in a timely fashion and that the schedule is realistic and allows for completion of the overall PBL project within the allocated time frame.

By thoroughly and carefully developing the project plan beforehand, using many of these instructional techniques, teachers can alleviate the sense of unease they may feel relative to who controls the classroom as they move into PBL. Students will be exercising much more control over what questions they ask, how they study given topics, and what activities they choose to complete, but the teacher can and will exercise control within the class, while freeing students to make some choices about their own learning.

Conclusions

This chapter and the previous chapter have presented many instructional options that can be implemented in the context of PBL, including options based in modern teaching technologies, as well as tried-and-true instructional assignments that are likewise found in most classrooms today. Each teacher will find his or her own comfort level within this array of instructional options and from that point will develop new professional instructional skills within the context of PBL project planning.

However, in addition to the primary task of instruction expected of all teachers, those educators likewise have the responsibility for evaluation and grading of students' work. While effective grading is always a challenge, evaluation and grading within the PBL paradigm nevertheless entails all of the options, with their respective advantages and disadvantages, as evaluation and grading within more traditional classrooms. The next chapter presents an array of grading options, based on the instructional suggestions presented herein, and should assist teachers in the evaluation and grading process in the context of PBL instruction.

6

Assessment Options for Project-Based Learning

Assessment within a PBL framework is somewhat different from assessment in more traditional educational paradigms, and for that reason many assessment alternatives are provided in virtually every discussion of PBL (Barell, 2007; Boss & Krauss, 2007; Larmer et al., 2009; Salend, 2009). First, because PBL emphasizes deeper conceptual understanding and problem solving, evaluations tend to be somewhat more reflective than in the more traditional classroom. While evaluation of recall for factual material is certainly a component of assessment within PBL as in all areas of education, other forms of assessment are used more frequently in PBL that emphasize deeper understanding, including self-reflection, portfolio assessment, authentic assessment, and peer evaluation, in addition to teacher evaluations.

> Because the emphasis within PBL involves deeper conceptual understanding and problem solving, evaluations tend to be somewhat more reflective than in the typical classroom.

Next, assessment within PBL work tends to be somewhat broader than that in the traditional classroom. Because PBL stresses skills for the 21st-century workplace, many aspects of assessment and evaluation of work are included herein that are not stressed as much in traditional instruction. For example, while rubrics are frequently used in classrooms today, these are stressed even more heavily in

PBL evaluations. In fact, rubrics seem to be the assessment practice that is most heavily emphasized in the PBL literature (Barell, 2007; Boss & Krauss, 2007; Larmer et al., 2009). Previous chapters of this text have presented various examples of rubrics, and the discussion that follows provides additional guidance on formulation of rubrics in the PBL context.

Next, PBL assessments frequently include various assessment alternatives such as self-assessment, peer assessment, or personal reflections because these reflective evaluations are quite common in many working environments today. Also, given a variety of assessment strategies that are recommended, it is likely that both individual and group grades (i.e., instances in which the same grade is awarded to each member of the group) will be found in most PBL units. In fact, most PBL projects result in an array of both individual and group grades, generated by different groups.

This variety of grading practices, coupled with the two types of grades (individual and group) makes the task of assigning a single semester grade to an individual student a bit more complex than in the traditional class where virtually all grades represent teacher evaluations of individual efforts. Teachers have to give some consideration to synthesizing grades from various individually created or group-created artifacts in most PBL projects.

> The use of both individual and group grades must be considered in PBL work, since most projects result in an array of both individual and group grades.

This chapter presents options for assessment and grading of both individual artifacts within a PBL project and group-produced artifacts, as well as options for assigning semester grades for the PBL project as a whole. First, the issue of content coverage and academic performance on Common Core State Standards (or state standards)—an issue critical for all teachers today—is briefly discussed in terms of how students respond to PBL instruction in statewide assessment programs.

Next, the use of rubrics is discussed. Of course, most teachers already use rubrics to some degree, and implementation of rubrics in PBL is not particularly different than in other instructional paradigms. Still, a template and guidelines for rubric development within PBL are presented. Next, the advantages of self-evaluation and peer evaluation are discussed along with suggestions for teachers to consider in using these evaluation formats. Portfolio assessment is discussed next, since many PBL projects do involve synthesis of more than one grade (i.e., there will probably be multiple grades for different artifacts), and portfolios provide one way to summarize a longer or larger body of work.

Finally, a section on grading PBL projects is presented. This involves practical suggestions on the mix of graded and nongraded work that might be included within a PBL project and suggestions for translating those grades into a semester grade.

Content Coverage Versus Learning in a Standards-Based Era

As briefly discussed in the earlier chapters, many teachers today feel pressure to cover the instructional standards represented within the Common Core State Standards (www.corestandards.org/the-standards) or the educational standards adopted for their state. Thus, teachers must plan the instruction units within a given semester or year to make certain that all of those topical standards are covered, and teachers are understandably concerned with how the issue of content coverage is addressed within PBL. In one sense, this can be considered the very essence of the teacher's job; this question represents the intersection of instruction and assessment. Is the teacher covering the content standards for his or her subject in such a way that state assessments demonstrate that students are meeting or exceeding achievement goals based on those standards?

This critical question can present a barrier to implementation of PBL if teachers feel that using a PBL instructional approach might prevent them from covering the content standards as required. Indeed, it was surprising to this author how few books or articles on PBL have addressed this critical question, a question near and dear to all teachers' hearts today. In order to explore this critical question in relation to assessment, educators must honestly consider what traditional instruction means in terms of "content coverage," how content coverage is related to student learning, and subsequently how the content coverage demand might play out within a PBL framework.

> The content coverage issue can present a barrier to implementation of PBL if teachers feel that using a PBL instructional approach might prevent them from covering the educational standards required.

In traditional instruction, teachers plan instructional units such that all chapters of the required text are assigned and taught within a given year, and to the degree that the selected text completely addresses state standards in a given content area, covering all of the chapters assures that all required content standards have been "taught" or covered. However, all veteran teachers would probably agree that there is a substantial difference between teaching a content standard (i.e., content coverage) and student mastery of that content standard, particularly for students struggling in a given class. In short, content coverage does not automatically equal learning in any instructional format, and that distinction is critical as teachers consider a move to PBL instruction.

It is clear that when teachers focus exclusively on content coverage, some students are likely to be left behind in terms of their mastery of specific topics during the semester or year. Teachers may feel pressure to move on to the next instructional unit to be covered within the year-long course, even while they realize that some students have not mastered the content of the instructional unit then under study. Of course, if that teacher moves into the next unit, some students may never master the content from the previous unit, and that academic deficit will show up for those students on the subsequent state assessments. Given the increased emphasis on standards-based instruction and content coverage since 2000, virtually all teachers in the classroom today have wrestled with that very issue.

> Teachers often feel pressure to move on to the next instructional unit to be covered within the year-long course, even while they realize that some students have not mastered the content of the instructional unit currently under study.

To consider content coverage in terms of a PBL-based curriculum, teachers must realize two things. First, in developing the PBL projects for the semester or year, all educational standards from the Common Core, or from state-approved curricula in a given state (since not all states have adopted the Common Core State Standards), can be addressed within the context of one PBL unit or another. As teachers map out five, six, or eight projects for a class to undertake throughout a given academic year, the teachers will map the Common Core State Standards or their state's educational standards (see the example in the appendix) across those PBL projects to assure content coverage, just as they have probably done when planning instructional units for that year. Thus, content coverage in PBL tends to be at least as thorough as in traditional instruction.

However, teachers should also realize a second point; their instruction is likely to result in increased achievement in PBL units because students are much more engaged in the curriculum. Research has painted a much stronger picture of the efficacy of PBL for teaching standards-based content. As reported previously, research has shown that PBL, when compared with more traditional standards-based instruction, results in higher academic achievement as shown on statewide, standards-based assessments (Boaler, 2002; Geier et al., 2008; Stepien et al., 1992; Strobel & van Barneveld, 2008).

Thus, teachers can rest assured that the assessment results for PBL-based instructional classes will show that enhanced achievement. Indeed, this research base is one of the major reasons that PBL is receiving increased emphasis throughout the United States and around the world. For that reason, teachers can feel confident in moving to PBL-based instruction that students, on average, will do better on statewide, standards-based assessments than they would in traditional classrooms.

> Higher student engagement in PBL results in much higher achievement than in traditional instruction, and assessment results for PBL-based instruction will show that enhanced achievement.

Rubrics Within PBL Projects

Rubrics have been used in classrooms for many years now, and numerous teachers are familiar with these instructional and assessment tools. Rubrics help structure assignments (as has been emphasized throughout this text) and can also be used to evaluate virtually all work in a PBL unit. Therefore, it should come as no surprise that many proponents of PBL recommend rubrics as perhaps one of the most important evaluation tools in PBL units (Barell, 2007; Boss & Krauss, 2007; Larmer et al., 2009). However, some teachers may not yet be aware of these tools so some background information may be necessary here.

In simple terms, a rubric is a scoring procedure or guide that lists specific criteria for student performance and in many cases describes different performance levels for those criteria. A good rubric should address all relevant components of an artifact or other type of assignment within a PBL project, as well as set specific criteria for students' work. Rubrics should be constructed to yield consistent results on the same product or artifact, even if the rubric-based evaluation is completed by different evaluators. Because of the high level of specificity required within rubrics, rubrics provide excellent guidance for student projects within the PBL framework, and for that reason, rubrics should be shared with the students before or as the PBL assignments are undertaken (Boss & Krauss, 2007).

> A rubric is a scoring procedure or guide that lists specific criteria for student performance and describes different performance levels for those criteria.

Beyond providing excellent guidance to students, however, rubrics hold several additional advantages. Good rubrics provide sufficient detail for individuals to self-evaluate their work during the development or work completion process. Rubrics also assist peers and teachers in making evaluation decisions. Because PBL instruction stresses motivation and self-direction more so than certain other types of traditional instruction, rubrics fit nicely within the PBL instructional approach (Barell, 2007; Belland et al., 2009; Boss & Krauss, 2007; Larmer et al., 2009). For example, Larmer et al. (2009) recommend that a rubric be devised and used for virtually every artifact or assignment within a PBL project. Further, in addition to using rubrics for evaluation of individual artifacts, rubrics may also be used, particularly in shorter PBL projects, as a mechanism for overall evaluation of the entire PBL project.

Various Types of Rubrics

Rubrics may be either holistic or analytic/descriptive (the website www.csufresno.edu/irap/assessment/rubric.shtml presents a nice description of these different types of rubrics). Essentially, a holistic rubric is typically designed to provide an overall rating on a student's work, and that rating is often associated with several discrete descriptors that, taken together, result in a single grade for that work. A rubric of this nature was presented in Box 4.3 previously in this book.

> A holistic rubric is typically designed to provide an overall rating on a student's work, and that rating is often associated with descriptors that, taken together, result in a single grade.

In contrast, an analytic rubric provides multiple indicators that enable analysis of various parts of the assignment as a whole. Further, most analytic rubrics likewise include some scale delineating levels of performance on each individual descriptor or component task (Salend, 2009). Because analytic rubrics provide more guidance for students, they are typically preferable to more holistic rubrics. Further, developing analytic rubrics for various PBL artifacts is not difficult, so the majority of rubrics developed and used by teachers are of this analytic or descriptive type.

In most cases, rubric development is completed in the PBL planning and design phase before the actual project begins in the classroom. Larmer et al. (2009) emphasize that teachers should plan PBL artifacts or projects as a whole with the end in mind. Thus, teachers should initiate a PBL project with a firm set of exact expectations relative to what students must do to complete the project, and this will of necessity involve careful planning of rubrics for assessing various artifacts well before a PBL unit is begun.

> An analytic rubric provides multiple indicators that enable analysis of various parts of the assignment as a whole.

Developing Rubrics

Analytic rubrics cross-reference various aspects of the task with assorted levels of performance (Barell 2007; Larmer et al., 2009). Box 1.3 in this book presented an analytic rubric associated with an entire PBL project. Of course, analytic rubrics may be quite complex, or relatively simple, and may be associated either with an entire project or with a specific artifact or task assignment within a PBL project.

As Box 1.3 shows, most rubrics may be pictured as a grid with task components, various task assignments, or different objectives listed down the side and levels of performance listed across the top. In Box 1.3 a four-by-four grid is pictured with four different assignment aspects listed on the left side and four different levels of performance listed across the top. Also, within each section of that grid, one may find specific indicators of task completion. While the number of assignments and levels of performance might vary from one rubric to another, the vast majority of rubrics are pictured as grids, with three, four, or five task components identified and three, four, or five different levels of performance delineated on top of the grid.

Box 6.1 presents another type of analytic rubric that allows teachers to evaluate individual aspects of the work without differentiating specific levels of performance. This rubric relates to evaluation of the PBL project described in Chapter 4, the Civil War memorial garden project. This rubric focuses on evaluation of the entire PBL proposal and could be used by either the teacher and peers in the final evaluation of the PBL projects within the class or by the Battlefield Commission in selecting a particular Civil War memorial garden design.

With these rubrics as examples, it is relatively easy to begin designing a rubric that will assist students in the learning process and serve as an evaluation or grading tool. There are a number of questions such as the following that will assist teachers in rubric design (Barell 2007; Larmer et al., 2009).

Box 6.1 Rubric for PBL Memorial Garden Design Project

Task Description: The students will develop a PowerPoint presentation (or similar multimedia presentation) that describes their proposal for the memorial garden project. Presentations should be approximately 10 to 15 minutes long.

Issue	Indicators	Evaluative Comments and Points Awarded
Knowledge of and sensitivity to background issues (20% of grade)	• Complete knowledge of slavery and other causes of the war shown • Representation of both Southern and Union perspectives • All required perspectives included	
Garden plan (40% of grade)	• A well-designed schematic of the proposed design is included • Design components thematically related to perspectives presented • Appropriate and pleasing artistic structure for the design as a whole is apparent • Both vertical and horizontal images incorporated within the plan	

Educational value
(20% of grade)

- The proposed plan is likely to result in increased understanding of the rich history of the battlefield area
- Historical facts presented to educate viewer on different perspectives
- Plan celebrates our common history by valuing all reasonable perspectives

Presentation impact
(10% of grade)

- This presentation is appropriate to use in other community presentation to solicit support for the plan
- Presenters made eye contact and answered questions directly and knowledgably
- Multimedia, digital images, art, and other visual aids were well developed and included as appropriate

Overall efficacy
(10% of grade)

- This presentation is convincing and compelling
- This presentation convinced me

- Is the rubric intended to evaluate an entire PBL project or merely one assignment or artifact within that project?
- How extensive can the rubric be?
- Can meaningful specific indicators be provided for the construct to be covered?
- What are the indicators, and how can I group them in a meaningful way?
- What scale do I wish to use for evaluation on each indicator?
- Should I relate that evaluation scale to the students' overall PBL grade and if so, how?

As these questions indicate, designing rubrics is not difficult, and veteran teachers may have designed many rubrics over the years. The two main components of a rubric are the evaluative indicators, placed in meaningful combinations, typically down the left side of the rubric, and the evaluation scale, which is typically pictured running across the top of the rubric grid. Instead of indicators on the left-hand side of the rubric, some rubrics present merely the names of specific aspects of the assignment or even the names of specific assignments within a broader PBL project. Box 6.2 presents several websites that offer additional assistance to teachers in developing rubrics for PBL teaching. Many of these websites include sample rubrics that teachers may retrieve and download as the basis or template for rubric development in their own class.

Box 6.2 Websites to Assist in Designing Rubrics

www.csufresno.edu/irap/assessment/rubric.shtml. This website stems from the California State University at Fresno. Sample rubrics are included for a variety of subjects including writing and language arts, and this website differentiated between holistic rubrics, resulting in a summative grade for a project, and analytic rubrics that involve deeper analysis of specific portions or segments within a PBL assignment.

www.educationworld.com/a_curr/curr248.shtmo. This site presents information on rubrics across the school age span, ranging from definition of a rubric to many sample rubrics. Also, the authors of this site recommend specific additional sites that will assist teachers in building rubrics.

(Continued)

Box 6.2 (Continued)

---

www.introductiontorubrics.com/samples.html. This website is associated with a book on rubrics and presents several sample rubrics as well as rubric templates for three, four, and five performance levels. Several different types of rubrics are presented, which will help teachers understand the assessment options that rubrics provide.

http://rubistar.4teachers.org. This website allows teachers to create a free rubric specifically for project-based learning projects. It was developed by the University of Kansas and will assist teachers in a variety of subject areas and topics including math, reading, writing, science, oral projects, and other topics. Also, this site includes an option for making your rubrics interactive, allowing the teacher to create detailed feedback for the students, and the interactive feature ties with other class management tools such as Moodle.

www.rubrics4teachers.com. This website is associated with the Western Governor's University site, Teacher Planet, and is intended to assists teachers with design and multimedia instruction, including rubric development. Many sample rubrics can be downloaded free and adapted for your particular use. Rubrics are provided in virtually all subject areas.

Reflective Self-Evaluation in PBL

As mentioned previously, PBL proponents tend to stress self-evaluation for students in PBL projects (Barell, 2007; Larmer et al., 2009; Partnership for 21st Century Skills, 2009). Self-evaluation skills tend to enhance students' work over time, and teaching them clearly prepares students for the world of work in the 21st century. For these reasons, reflective self-evaluation tends to be emphasized more in PBL than in more traditional instruction (Barell, 2007; Larmer et al., 2009).

Chapter 1, for example, presented the option of reflective self-evaluation via student journaling in a PBL project. Journaling does create an atmosphere in which students can reflect on their learning, and when the teacher and student discuss the student's journal entries together, those entries can provide some basis for self-evaluation or even for specific grades. However, there are at least two perspectives on the use of journal entries in grading. One perspective suggests that journal entries should be used as a point of reflection and as a basis of discussion with the teacher, but they should not be used to generate a grade. This perspective suggests that one major aim of journaling is to encourage free-flowing thought and that assigning grades to journals might restrict that thought process for some students. Other teachers, however, take a different perspective and do assign grades for journal entries. This, of course, is a professional decision for the teacher to make, and there is no "wrong" perspective on that question. However, should a teacher wish to preserve journaling as a nongraded assignment with a PBL project, there are other self-reflection options that can be used for grading in that same project, as discussed now.

Numeric Self-Evaluations in PBL

Some teachers choose to use a numeric scale on which students rate their own work, and such a self-reflective rating can easily be translated into grades. For example, a simple, numerically based Likert scale evaluation can be of great benefit for students in helping them evaluate their work on an artifact or within a PBL project overall. An example is presented in Box 6.3.

More so than a journal item entry, a numeric scale evaluation such as this encourages students to not only evaluate their work but determine in a relative sense the overall quality of their work in specific areas. When an indicator about one's work is considered by a student, relative to the "excellent" criteria as expressed on the evaluation in Box 6.3 (i.e., could not have been done any better), students tend to more accurately determine the worth of their effort and work overall. Of course, many students will inflate their grade somewhat, while others may grade themselves a bit too harshly, but those evaluations merely represent opportunities for the teacher to discuss the quality of the work with the students in question, as well as coach those students in self-evaluation.

Note that the directions for this self-evaluation indicate that points will be awarded to the student based on his or her agreement with the teacher on the evaluation items. That type of reward structure tends to increase student accuracy in these self-evaluation tasks. Also, having students sign the bottom of these evaluations is recommended, as that practice can increase the students' sense of

Box 6.3 A Numerically Based Likert Scale Self-Evaluation

Please rate yourself on the questions below, with a 5 indicating excellent, or "couldn't be done any better," and a 1 indicating "needs considerable improvement." Your teacher will discuss your evaluations with you when you finish, and points will be awarded when your assessment agrees with the teacher's assessment on the same question.

Student name _____ **Date of self-evaluation** _____

Name of the assignment evaluated _____

I researched this topic completely in the time given.	1	2	3	4	5
This assignment presents multiple research sources.	1	2	3	4	5
I present a reasonable set of summaries of the information.	1	2	3	4	5
My work on this synthesizes this information well.	1	2	3	4	5
This work shows critical evaluation of the evidence.	1	2	3	4	5
I present various sides of the argument or evidence.	1	2	3	4	5
My work is neat, clear, and understandable.	1	2	3	4	5
This work is presented in the most appropriate format.	1	2	3	4	5
Overall I would evaluate my work on this as:	1	2	3	4	5

Signature:
By signing this work, you are indicating that this is an honest, accurate evaluation. The teacher will review and discuss this evaluation with you and sign below after that meeting.

Teacher signature _____

169

the importance of the evaluations. In fact, requiring a signature helps students, even in lower grades, understand that they are committed to do their best.

One additional advantage of numeric self-evaluations involves the necessity to generate grades on individual assignments or on the PBL project as a whole. It is much easier to transfer numeric scale evaluation information to a numeric grade on the project when compared to a set of self-reflective journal statements. Of course, grading should not be the main priority in self-evaluation, but the task of grading is nevertheless often necessary at the end of PBL projects when grades must be generated for all students. Thus, many teachers include numeric, Likert scale student evaluations within the overall PBL project.

Open-Ended Self-Evaluations in PBL

While a Likert scale can assist students in reflecting on their work on the specific indicators in question, it may not show how or why they evaluated themselves as they did on any particular indicator. Thus, some teachers prefer more open-ended self-evaluation questions that elicit a specific answer from students on one or more aspects of their work. These might be questions such as why a student believes that he or she succeeded in an assignment or how that work might be improved. In that sense, open-ended questions in which a student has to construct a written answer are the most useful form of self-evaluation. Like the numeric scale evaluation already described, this type of evaluation item will cause the student to reflect more deeply on a specific aspect of his or her work. An open-ended self-evaluation of this nature is presented in Box 6.4.

Of course, the self-evaluation tools used in PBL will vary considerably from project to project or from grade to grade, and teachers are not limited to these three self-evaluation options (journaling, numeric scale evaluations, or open-ended questions). For example, teachers may wish to combine numeric, Likert scale items and open-ended questions on a self-evaluation in order to best assist the student in evaluating his or her work. While many options exist, teachers should remember one imperative: in PBL, reflective self-evaluation is strongly encouraged, since this teaches a self-evaluation skill that, in most cases, enhances performance and directly transfers to the world of work in the 21st century.

Box 6.4 Questions for a Self-Evaluation

1. Have I listed at least three content points, aspects, or ideas within the content that this artifact should display in some fashion? List these below.

   _____

2. Is this artifact complete? What should be added?

   _____

3. Can I add any information to this without it being too much?

   _____

4. Could I display those concepts in some other fashion more easily? What other format could I use?

   _____

5. Is this project neat and clear to the viewer? Are there ambiguities in this work?

   _____

6. Are the concepts displayed here related to each other, and are those relationships clear in this artifact?

   _____

7. Does this artifact reflect work that I will be proud for the entire school *community to see?*

   _____

8. Based on the answers to these questions, what numeric grade would I assign myself on this artifact, using a scale of 0 to 100, with 100 representing a perfect assignment that could not be improved upon?

   _____

Reflective Peer Evaluations

Another evaluation option that is typically included in PBL projects is the use of peer evaluations (Barell, 2007; Boss & Krause, 2007; Larmer et al., 2009). While peer evaluations are not essential for all PBL projects, they are recommended in much of the PBL literature (Baron, 2011; David, 2008; Ghosh, 2010; Larmer & Mergendoller, 2010). As students engage in more team-based PBL instructional tasks, they often begin to offer each other informal feedback within their instructional teams, even when no formal peer evaluation is called for. The very nature of the PBL experience makes nearly all students want to improve the PBL products by helping their teammates within the PBL group, and peer evaluation can be viewed as an extension of that naturally occurring phenomenon (Belland et al., 2009; Laboy-Rush, 2011; Mergendoller et al., 2007).

> As students engage in more team-based PBL experiences, they often begin to offer each other informal feedback within their instructional teams even when no formal feedback is called for.

However, when teachers choose to use peer evaluations they must be carefully cognizant of the fact that some students have not evaluated their peers previously and may not have the specific skills necessary for effective peer evaluations. Thus, teachers who wish to use peer evaluation will need to teach these skills in the first several PBL projects. Some general guidelines for completing peer evaluations are presented in Box 6.5, and teachers may adapt these and use them for that instruction as necessary. Of course, like many of these 21st-century group-task skills, these workplace skills will become more ingrained as students work more in the PBL format. Thus students become increasingly competent at conducting meaningful peer evaluations.

Box 6.5 Guidelines for Peer Evaluations

In conducting peer evaluations, the sole focus should be on providing assistance to the student or group of students that developed the product, report, presentation, or artifact. Always remember that our goal in peer evaluations is to support those students and offer our best advice about how their product might be improved. Remember that we are critiquing the product and not the student or students who developed the product. Here are some guidelines that should help.

1. Always review the product or artifact carefully in completing your evaluation.

(Continued)

Box 6.5 (Continued)

2. Next, prepare written evaluation remarks prior to talking with the student whose work you are evaluating. That lets you review the remarks and points in order to check them and to remove any harsh criticism.

3. Always seek some positive things to say initially. That helps in getting the evaluation discussion going and makes negative critique points easier to discuss.

4. State even the negative discussion points as positively as you can whenever possible. Example: "While I liked the way you did _____, I was concerned with one aspect of that."

5. Be specific in both positive and negative comments. Examples: "That was a great segment of the digital video when you discussed _____ (topic here)." "I feel that this could have been done better if you had also presented information on _____."

6. Be succinct in your comments. Generally a paragraph of six to ten sentences is more than long enough to note both the strengths and weaknesses of an artifact.

7. Be prepared to explain any negative comments and give examples of what you believe will improve the artifact.

8. After your comments are prepared in writing, share them with the teacher and seek guidance on how the phrasing might be improved. Then share that evaluation with the student.

9. Never engage in debate about the points you make. While always allowing students to make comments relative to your critique, you should refer any serious evaluation disagreements to the teacher.

With those guidelines for peer evaluations noted, teachers may feel free to implement either a numeric scale peer evaluation, an open-ended question type of peer evaluation, or a combination of the two. Box 6.6 presents a template for peer evaluation using a Likert scale, and teachers should note the obvious similarities between this evaluation and the Likert scale evaluation in Box 6.3. As shown here, once the indicators for the evaluation have been developed by the teacher, it is a fairly simple procedure to revise those only slightly and change them from a self-evaluation indicator to a peer evaluation indicator.

Box 6.6 Sample Likert Scale Peer Evaluation

Please rate the work of _____ on the questions that follow, with a 5 indicating excellent, or "couldn't be done any better," and a 1 indicating "needs considerable improvement." Your teacher will discuss your evaluations with you when you finish, and points will be awarded when your assessment agrees with the teacher's assessment on the same question.

Student or PBL group name _____ **Date** _____

Name of the assignment evaluated _____

This person or PBL group:

Researched this topic completely	1	2	3	4	5
Presented multiple research sources	1	2	3	4	5
Presented a reasonable set of summaries of the information	1	2	3	4	5
Synthesized this information well	1	2	3	4	5
Showed critical evaluation of the evidence	1	2	3	4	5
Presented various sides of the argument or evidence	1	2	3	4	5
Prepared work that was neat, clear, and understandable	1	2	3	4	5
Presented the work in the most appropriate format	1	2	3	4	5
Overall I would evaluate this work as	1	2	3	4	5

Signature:
By signing this work, you are indicating that this is an honest, accurate evaluation. The teacher will review and discuss this evaluation with you and sign below after that meeting.

Teacher signature _____

Further, as in the self-evaluation arena, teachers may choose to provide a more open-ended form of evaluation questionnaire for peer evaluation. Peer evaluation questions will vary from one project or artifact to the next, and teachers should modify these indicators as necessary given the specific PBL project, but the indicators presented in Box 6.7 can serve as a guide for this open-ended peer evaluation.

Box 6.7 Peer Evaluation Form

1. Is a list of content items prepared that is to be shown by this artifact?

   _____

2. Given that list of ideas or concepts, is this artifact complete?

   _____

3. Should additional information be included here? If so, what?

   _____

4. Should this information be presented in some other type of artifact or in some other fashion? If so, what do we suggest?

   _____

5. Is this project neat and are the concepts clear?

   _____

6. Are the concepts displayed here related to each other? Are those relationships clear in this artifact?

   _____

7. Does this artifact reflect work that our class will be proud to share with the entire school community?

   _____

8. What is the best advice I (we) can offer this student(s) for improvement of this product?

   _____

9. Based on these evaluation points, what numeric grade would I assign this project, with 100 reflecting a perfect grade?

   _____

Portfolio Assessment

Another form of assessment that tends to be stressed in PBL work is the use of portfolios (Barell, 2007; Salend, 2009). Larmer et al. (2009) suggest that, rather than assigning one grade for a PBL project overall, teachers should formulate several grades with various grades associated with separate artifacts within the larger PBL project. Further, they recommend a mix of individual and group grades, since that mix tends to emphasize both self-evaluation and the skills associated with evaluation of one's peers.

With this multigrade option in mind, portfolio assessment seems to be a natural option for PBL projects. A portfolio is more than merely a collection of a student's work. Rather, a portfolio represents a planned, structured effort to present the most accurate picture of student achievement possible by including a variety of work samples and looking at them as a whole in an effort to identify strengths and weaknesses to facilitate student improvement. Typically portfolios may include an index of the work samples that are included as well as evaluation comments relative to that work or to the overall collection of work.

> A portfolio is a planned, structured effort to present the most accurate picture of student achievement possible by including a variety of work samples and looking at them as a whole in an effort to identify strengths and weaknesses to facilitate student improvement.

In the context of a typical PBL project, students are likely to have many work samples and thus many evaluations included in the portfolio. Some evaluations may be based on self-evaluation of individual artifacts (as reviewed and amended by the teacher), others based on peer evaluation of specific assignments and artifacts, others on teacher-developed rubrics associated with particular products, and still others on the ultimate impact of the final PBL product (i.e., was the project recommendation adopted by the community in some form?). A portfolio allows teacher and student to develop a folder with multiple items included from a given PBL project, and evaluation of that work as a whole, to devise a semester grade.

Alternatively, portfolios can be used that include work from various PBL projects over time. For example, if a fifth-grade math class undertakes two different PBL projects during a nine-week grading period, items from both of those projects may be included within the portfolio for a particular student. Again, the portfolio emphasis is to most accurately represent the student's work, and in most portfolios, sample items may be either included or removed by the student and teacher in order to accurately reflect that work. For example, if a student in this math class did particularly well on a creative work assignment in the first project, but not the second, perhaps the creative endeavor from the second project would be removed from the portfolio, while the first creative product and its evaluation would be left in.

Of course, including or excluding work from the portfolio is at the joint discretion of the student and teacher. However, as this discussion emphasizes, portfolios do provide great flexibility as well as regular opportunities for teachers to discuss the work with individual students on a repeated basis. In that fashion, teachers tend to talk more frequently with students about their work when portfolios are used, and that will tend to stress the importance of the work. For many students, that extra notice can be the catalyst for more serious attention to their studies.

Grading PBL Work

Celebration! The Essence of Authentic Assessment

Traditionally, grading practices in schools have represented everything but a celebration of student work. Grades were most frequently assigned by the teacher and based on teacher evaluation, and while higher grades within a classroom may have been mentioned positively or higher achievement praised in some fashion, achievement for most students in the schools has typically not been celebrated to any degree.

Happily, PBL holds the promise of reversing that fact (Boss & Krauss, 2007). PBL stresses the "authenticity" of the work that students undertake by associating work with real-world problems and, once problem solutions are generated, by having students present those problem solutions and answers in some published format. Thus, both teachers and students tend to value—to celebrate— student work more in the PBL paradigm than in traditional instruction. In fact, one would be hard-pressed to devise a more authentic work assignment than the example presented for planning a Civil War memorial garden described in this book. In that example, students were actually presenting their suggestions and garden plans to the group that had called for community assistance. In that sense, the students were doing "real" work that would benefit their local community, work that could have and might have been undertaken by a landscape planning firm on a fee-for-service basis had the students not completed that work.

When the final collective work of the students involves some form of publication in some important venue, that can represent the most authentic form of evaluation. That work is celebrated by the presentation of the end product in that public forum. In short, one can ask the question, "Were the students' ideas represented in that work adopted by an agency of the community?" Further, the answer to that question can serve as, for some students, the most important evaluation or "grade" that they ever receive. If a problem solution generated by students helps the community, then that "evaluation" truly can become a celebration of students' learning (Boss & Krauss, 2007).

Again, one strength of PBL is the possibility of teaching in a format that uses authentic problems in order to excite students about their learning. If educators wish to excite young minds, and tap that wonderful resource of student capability to address problems and issues within the community, the PBL can be the vehicle for celebration of the worth of the work students undertake.

Thus, where considering grading in the PBL context, the educator's first question should be, "How can we collectively devise an evaluation and grading format that will lead to celebration of students' work?" In that context, various options for grading, including many of those discussed, will fit more easily into place and will seem much more appropriate than a teacher assigning a grade based exclusively on a student's class assignments.

A Plethora of Grading Options

Within the context of that question, the array of options discussed in this chapter can provide some alternatives. Of course, even with celebration of student work as the primary goal, teachers will still ultimately face the rather mundane task of assigning a grade to individual students, and no discussion of PBL instruction is complete without some consideration of how final grades might be administered within the PBL framework.

In PBL projects, as in life, much of the work is collaborative, and this might suggest that a single grade awarded to all group members is appropriate. However, some of the work on specific artifacts will be individual, suggesting the use of individual grades for those assignments. Further, depending on the desires and planning of the teacher and the students, additional individual projects can be built into the broader PBL task, and those will need some type of grade as well.

Therefore, there will be ample opportunity for both individual and group grades throughout the PBL experience.

While group grades (i.e., the same grade given to each member of a project or PBL team) will stress the collaborative nature of the broad PBL task, it is frequently advantageous for teachers to likewise consider awarding individual grades. In particular, in cases where one or two team members are predominately responsible for creating an artifact for the entire group, or completing a certain assignment, those individuals might be awarded individual grades by the teacher, which should be reflective of their individual contributions. Thus, in light of this discussion, most proponents of PBL recommend a mix of both individual and group grades within a given PBL project (Larmer et al., 2009).

Generating Semester or Project Grades

With this array of grading possibilities the generation of a specific semester grade for an individual student can seem to be a daunting task. Of course any and all of the assessment options described in this chapter can and should be used for assigning numeric grades for specific tasks within the overall PBL project. Ultimately, however, teachers are responsible for assigning final grades in their classrooms. Thus, in most cases, when a class reaches the end of a multiweek PBL project, teachers are left with the task of synthesizing a variety of both group grades on specific assignments and individual grades on other assignments in order to generate each student's individual grade for the semester or grading period. Teachers will need to generate some type of weighted grade schedule for the PBL project overall. Therefore, a grade on a six- to twelve-week PBL project in a given class would probably represent some method by which individual grades on various assessments are compiled, resulting in a numeric grade for each individual student's report card.

As the sample PBL project in Chapter 4 demonstrated, PBL projects do include a number of evaluations of various artifacts. In that project, students were given some choice of assignments to complete, but that PBL project included 13 specific artifacts or assignments given for each group, though some of these were not graded. Box 6.8 presents those assignments and indicates who was responsible for assigning a grade, the mechanism (e.g., was a rubric available?), and the type of grade—individual, partner, or group grade—that would be assigned.

Box 6.8 Artifacts/Assignments and a Student's Grades

Type of Assignment	Grading Process	Type of Grade
Three webquests	Rubrics provided (graded by teacher)	Three grades (same grade for all partners)
Jigsaw activity	Nongraded	
Participation in class wiki	Nongraded	
Digital journal	Nongraded	
Character biography	Rubric provided (graded by teacher)	One individual grade
Flight to Freedom game	Nongraded	
One or two creative products	Peer evaluations	Two group grades
Two planning artifacts	Nongraded	
Memorial garden diagram	Peer evaluation with rubric	Common group grade
PowerPoint presentation and garden recommendation	Teacher evaluation	Common group grade Counted twice

As Box 6.8 indicates, there are seven numeric grades in that project, though students could opt out of some of the graded assignments. However, each student would have a minimum of six numeric grades, some of which were generated by teacher evaluation and some by peer evaluation using various rubrics. Some of these reflect grades on group work, while others are partner or individual grades. In order to synthesize these grades and generate individual student grades for a report card at the end of the semester, the grading description within the project itself (see Box 4.9) indicated that all grades would be compiled on a 0–100 point scale and then averaged. However, this would be a weighted average in that the grade for the culminating project would be added in twice in the final grade calculation for each student. While this sounds somewhat complicated, in reality teachers complete this type of semester-end grading very frequently. In the case of PBL, however, the grades are much more likely to reflect peer evaluation information or, in other cases, self-evaluation information as well as teacher-generated grades.

Conclusions

In the context of the instructional options presented in Chapters 3 and 4, teachers embarking on PBL instruction will face many interesting questions relative to both instruction and assessment. While most teachers have had experience with using rubrics, portfolios, or perhaps even self-evaluation or peer evaluation in the class, placing these in the context of PBL instruction does result in an increased emphasis on these grading and evaluation paradigms, approaches that have been less frequently used in traditional classrooms. This chapter has presented guidelines for all of these evaluation and assessment options, as well as suggestions on how these grading practices may be fitted together in the PBL context.

In a broader sense, this book has endeavored to show how PBL can be implemented within the next decade. With increased emphasis in the educational literature on authentic learning, technology in the classroom, and project-based problem solving, PBL is receiving increasing attention as the teaching paradigm of the future. While PBL can be incorporated into the instructional unit-based planning teachers use today, the book has also discussed PBL as a replacement for unit-based instruction. In fact, this author recommends PBL as an instructional approach in which all content is taught via PBL projects, with careful attention to mapping the Common Core State Standards or state standards across PBL units in a given subject area for a given academic year.

As the research reviewed herein indicates, the PBL instructional approach has been shown to be more effective than more traditional instruction, and that results from the higher levels of student engagement within the PBL paradigm (Geier et al., 2008; Stepien et al., 1992; Strobel & van Barneveld, 2008). Thus, both the enhanced academic performance associated with PBL, plus the fact that PBL stresses 21st-century workplace skills more so than traditional instruction, suggest that PBL should be one of the main instructional methods, if not *the* instructional method, for differentiating instruction in order to meet the needs of all students. Educators today are encouraged to explore and ultimately implement PBL instruction, as this truly represents 21st-century teaching at its finest. PBL is the best teaching practice for the new millennium.

Appendix

The Relationship Between PBL and State Curricular Standards

While many states have adopted or are currently moving toward adoption of the Common Core State Standards (www .corestandards.org/the-standards), some states such as Texas have chosen not to adopt these standards. This appendix is intended to demonstrate that various PBL assignments are well designed to address various standards from states that have not adopted the Common Core State Standards. While space precludes developing lists of all applicable standards from all states not adopting the Common Core State Standards, this appendix will focus on the Texas Essential Knowledge and Skills (TEKS) standards, and this example should suffice to demonstrate the applicability of PBL instruction for teaching various sets of educational standards in different states.

Common Core State Standards were mentioned in both Chapters 2 and 3, but they were discussed at length in Chapter 4 in relationship to a webquest dealing with American history and, in particular, the Civil War. As described, that webquest required application of various technologies such as development of a multimedia presentation, use of technology tools for research, and synthesis and evaluation of information from various sources.

The TEKS standards that follow were obtained from the Texas Education Agency website (http://ritter.tea.state.tx.us/rules/tac/chapter113/ch113b.html#113.18). The PBL lesson described in Chapter 4 required the type of synthesis of information represented by these standards for Grade 6 (identified as §Number 113.18, Social Studies, Grade 6, Beginning with School Year 2011–2012 at the website just listed).

(21) Social studies skills. The student applies critical-thinking skills to organize and use information acquired through established research methodologies from a variety of valid sources, including electronic technology. The student is expected to:

(A) differentiate between, locate, and use valid primary and secondary sources such as computer software; interviews; biographies; oral, print, and visual material; and artifacts to acquire information about various world cultures;

(B) analyze information by sequencing, categorizing, identifying cause-and-effect relationships, comparing, contrasting, finding the main idea, summarizing, making generalizations and predictions, and drawing inferences and conclusions;

(C) organize and interpret information from outlines, reports, databases, and visuals, including graphs, charts, timelines, and maps.

In addition to these skills, the PBL assignment on the Civil War described at length in Chapter 4 also requires students to evaluate and synthesize information from a variety of sources and to apply technology as a research tool in the area of social studies. These skills are identified within the TEKS standards as follows (identified as Number §113.39, Social Studies Research Methods—One-Half Credit on the website listed):

(3) Social studies skills. The student understands the fundamental principles and requirements of validity and reliability (both social science and historical fields of inquiry). The student is expected to:

(A) define and differentiate reliability and validity;

(B) identify methods of checking for reliability; and

(C) evaluate various sources for reliability and validity and justify the conclusions.

(4) Social studies skills. The student understands how data can be collected from a variety of sources using a variety of methods. The student is expected to:

(A) collect information from a variety of sources (primary, secondary, written, and oral) using techniques such as questionnaires, interviews, and library research; and

(B) use various technology such as CD-ROM, library topic catalogues, networks, and on-line information systems to collect information about a selected topic.

As this brief discussion shows, assignments within PBL units can be constructed to teach educational standards from virtually any list of standards that might be adopted by various states. In this text alone, educational standards have been presented from a variety of different sources (Common Core State Standards, Educational Technology Standards, and the Texas Education Agency), and many other states and organizations likewise promote various educational standards. The point here is that with a bit of teacher reflection, virtually any educational standard can be effectively addressed via PBL instruction.

References

Adams, D. M., & Hamm, M. (1994). *New designs for teaching and learning.* San Francisco: Jossey-Bass.

Ash, K. (2011). Games and simulations help children access science. *Education Week, 30*(27), 12.

Barell, J. (2007). *Problem-based learning: An inquiry approach* (2nd ed.). Thousand Oaks, CA: Corwin.

Barell, J. (2010). Problem-based learning: The foundation for 21st century skills. In J. Bellanca & R. Brandt (Eds.), *21st century skills: Rethinking how students learn.* Bloomington, IN: Solution Tree Press.

Baron, K. (2011). *Six steps for planning a successful project.* Retrieved on March 29, 2011, from www.edutopia.org/maine-project-learning-six-steps-planning

Bell, S. (2008, November/December). Wikis as legitimate research sources. *Online, 32*(6), 34–37.

Belland, B. R., French, B. F., & Ertmer, P. A. (2009). Validity and problem-based learning research: A review of instruments used to assess intended learning outcomes. *Interdisciplinary Journal of Problem-Based Learning, 3*(1), 59–89.

Bender, W. N., & Crane, D. (2011). *Response to intervention in mathematics.* Bloomington, IN: Solution Tree Press.

Bender, W. N., & Waller, L. (2011). *The teaching revolution: How RTI, technology, and differentiated instruction are restructuring teaching in the 21st century.* Thousand Oaks, CA: Corwin.

Blumenfeld, P. C., Soloway, E., Marx, R. W., Krajcik, J. S., Guzdial, M., & Palincsar, A. (1991). Motivating project-based learning: Sustaining the doing, supporting the learning. *Educational Psychologist, 26*(3,4), 369–398.

Boaler, J. (2002). Learning from teaching: Exploring the relationship between reform curriculum and equity. *Journal for Research in Mathematics Education, 33*(4), 239–258.

Bonk, C. (2010, June 1). *The flat world has swung open: How web technology is revolutionizing education.* Keynote presented at the Great Technology Stimulus Conference. Hosted by Region 17 Education Service Center, Lubbock, TX.

Boss, S., & Krauss, J. (2007). *Reinventing project-based learning: Your field guide to real-world projects in the digital age.* Washington, DC: International Society for Technology in Education.

Bransford, J., Brown, A., & Cocking, R. R. (Eds.). (2000). *How people learn— Brain, mind, experience, and school.* Washington, DC: National Academy Press.

Bransford, J. D., Sherwood, R. S., Vye, N. J., & Rieser, J. (1986). Teaching thinking and problem solving: Research foundations. *American Psychologist, 41,* 1078–1089.

Chapman, C., & King, R. (2005). *Differentiated assessment strategies: One tool doesn't fit all.* Thousand Oaks, CA: Corwin.

Cognition and Technology Group at Vanderbilt. (1992a). Anchored instruction in science and mathematics: Theoretical basis, developmental projects, and initial research findings. In R. A. Duschl & R. J. Hamilton (Eds.), *Philosophy of science, cognitive psychology, and educational theory and practice* (pp. 245–273). New York: State University of New York Press.

Cognition and Technology Group at Vanderbilt (CTGV). (1992b). The Jasper experiment: An exploration of issues in learning and instructional design. *Educational Technology Research and Development, 40,* 65–80.

Cole, J. E., & Wasburn-Moses, L. H. (2010). Going beyond "the math wars." A special educator's guide to understanding and assisting with inquiry-based teaching in mathematics. *Teaching Exceptional Children, 42*(4), 14–21.

Cote, D. (2007). Problem-based learning software for students with disabilities. *Intervention in School and Clinic, 43*(1), 29–37.

David, J. L. (2008). Project-based learning. *Teaching Students to Think, 66*(5), 80–82.

Davis, M. R. (2010, March 18). Solving algebra on smartphones. *Education Week, 29*(26), 20–23.

Dewey, J. (1933). *How we think.* Lexington, MA: D. C. Heath.

Drake, K., & Long, D. (2009). Rebecca's in the dark: A comparative study of problem-based learning and direct instruction/experiential learning in two 4th grade classrooms. *Journal of Elementary Science Education, 21*(1), 1–16.

Eicher, L. (2010). Educational video games gain acceptance as an effective response to intervention tool. *Tabula Digita.* Retrieved on June 28, 2010, from http://haoodnla.com/article/lyx09213342y9.01/413080

Fernando, A. (2007). Working off the same page. *Communication World, 24*(3), 11–13.

Ferriter, W. M., & Garry, A. (2010). *Teaching the iGeneration: 5 easy ways to introduce essential skills with web 2.0 tools.* Bloomington, IN: Solution Tree Press.

Fleischner, J., & Manheimer, M. (1997). Mathematics interventions for students with learning disabilities. Myths and realities. *School Psychology Review, 26*(3), 397–414.

Fortus, D., Krajcikb, J., Dershimerb, R. C., Marx, R. W., & Mamlok-Naamand, R. (2005). Design-based learning meets case-based reasoning in the middle-school science classroom. Putting learning by design into practice. *The Journal of the Learning Sciences,* 495–547.

Frontline. (2010, February 2). *Digital nation.* A PBS documentary. Retrieved on November 15, 2011, from www.pbs.org/wghb/pages/frontline

Geier, R., Blumenfeld, P. C., Marx, R. W., Krajcik, J. S., Fishman, B., Soloway, E., et al. (2008). Standardized test outcomes for students engaged in inquiry-based science curricula in the context of urban reform. *Journal of Research in Science Teaching, 45*(8), 922–939.

Ghosh, O. (2010). *Project based learning.* Retrieved on October 9, 2010, from www.buzzle.com/articles/problem-based-learning.html.

Gijbels, D., Dochy, F., Van den Bossche, P., & Segers, M. (2005). Effects of problem-based learning: A meta-analysis from the angle of assessment. *Review of Educational Research, 75*(1), 27–61.

Grant, M. M. (2010). *Getting a grip on project-based learning: Theory, cases and recommendations.* Retrieved on October 26, 2010, from www.ncsu.edu/meridian/winn2002/514/3.html

Hickey, D. T., Petrosino, A. J., Pellegrino, J. W., Goldman, S. R., Bransford, J. D., Sherwood, R., & the Cognition and Technology Group at Vanderbilt. (1994). The MARS mission challenge: A generative, problem-solving, school science environment. In S. Vosniadou, E. De Corte, & H. Mandl (Eds.), *Technology-based learning environments: Psychological and educational foundations* (NATO ASI series; pp. 97–103). New York: Springer-Verlag.

Huber, C. (2010). Professional learning 2.0. *Educational Leadership, 67*(8), 41–46.

Johnson, D. W., & Johnson, R. T. (1999). Theory into practice. *College of Education: Ohio University, 38*(2). Retrieved from www.fed.cuhk.edu.hk/staff/paper/mmchiu/EDU3310/JohnsonJohnson%20-%20Make%20CL%20work.pdf

Johnson, D. W., & Johnson, R. T. (2010). Cooperative learning and conflict resolution: Essential skills in the 21st century. In J. Bellanca & R. Brandt (Eds.), *21st century skills: Rethinking how students learn.* Bloomington, IN: Solution Tree Press.

Johnson, D.W., Johnson, R. T., & Smith, K. A. (1991). *Cooperative learning: Increasing college faculty instruction productivity.* Washington, DC: ASHE-ERIC Higher Education Report No. 4, George Washington University.

Johnson, D. W., Johnson, R. T., & Smith, K. A. (2007). The state of cooperative learning in postsecondary and professional settings. *Educational Psychology Review, 19*(1), 15–29.

Knowlton, D. (2003). Preparing students for enhanced living. In D. Knowlton & D. Sharp (Eds.), *Problem-based learning for the information age.* San Francisco: Jossey-Bass.

Laboy-Rush, D. (2011). *Integrating STEM education through project-based learning.* Paper retrieved on March 29, 2011, from http://learning.com/pdfs/STEM-White-Paper-101207.pdf

Land, S. M., & Green, B. A. (2000). Project-based learning with the World Wide Web: A qualitative study of resource integration. *Educational Technology Research and Development, 48*(1), 45–67.

Larmer, J., & Mergendoller, J. R. (2010). 7 Essentials for project-based learning. *Educational Leadership, 68*(1), 34–37.

Larmer, J., Ross, D., & Mergendoller, J. R. (2009). *PBL starter kit: To-the-point advice, tools, and tips for your first project in middle or high school.* San Rafael, CA: Unicorn Printing Specialists.

Levstik, L. S., & Barton, K. C. (2001). *Doing history.* Mahwah, NJ: Lawrence Erlbaum.

Maloney, D. H. (2010). Solving problems that count. *Educational Leadership, 68*(1), 55–58.

Manzo, K. K. (2010, March 18). Mobile learning seen to lack rigorous research. *Education Week, 29*(26), 34–36.

Marx, R. W., Blumenfeld, P. C., Krajcik, J. S., & Soloway, E. (1997). Enacting project-based science. *The Elementary School Journal, 97*(4), 341–358.

Marzano, R. J. (2007). *The art and science of teaching: A comprehension framework for effective instruction.* Alexandria, VA: Association for Supervision and Curriculum Development.

Marzano, R. J. (2009). Teaching with interactive whiteboards. *Educational Leadership, 87*(3), 80–82.

Marzano, R. J., & Haystead, M. (2009). *Final report on the evaluation of the Promethean technology.* Englewood, CO: Marzano Research Laboratory.

Marzano, R. J., Pickering, D. J., & Pollock, J. E. (2001). *Classroom instruction that works: Research-based strategies for increasing student achievement.* Alexandria, VA: Association for Supervision and Curriculum Development.

Mergendoller, J. R., Maxwell, N., & Bellisimo, Y. (2007). The effectiveness of problem based instruction: A comparative study of instructional methods and student characteristics. *Interdisciplinary Journal of Problem-Based Learning, 1*(2), 49–69.

Ogle, D. (1986). K-W-L: A teaching model that develops active reading of expository text. *Reading Teacher, 19*, 564–571.

Okolo, C. M., Englert, C. S., Bouck, E. C., & Heutsche, A. M. (2007). Web-based history learning environments: Helping all students learn and like history. *Intervention in School and Clinic, 43*(1), 3–11.

O'Meara, J. (2010). *Beyond differentiated instruction.* Thousand Oaks, CA: Corwin.

Partnership for 21st Century Skills. (2004). *Framework for 21st century learning.* Retrieved on September 9, 2010, from www.p21.org/index.php?option=com_content&task=view&id=254&Itemid=120

Partnership for 21st Century Skills. (2007). *21st century curriculum and instruction.* Retrieved on November 18, 2009, from www.21stcenturyskills.org/documents/21st_century_skills_curriculum_and_instruction.pdf

Partnership for 21st Century Skills. (2009). *21st century learning environments.* Retrieved on November 18, 2009, from www.21stcenturyskills.org/documents/1e_white_paper-1.pdf

Perkins, D. (1992). *Smart schools.* New York: Basic Books.

Petrosino, A. J. (1995). *Mission to Mars: An integrated curriculum.* Nashville, TN: The Cognition and Technology Group at Vanderbilt University.

Rhem, J. (1998). Project based learning: An introduction. *National Teaching and Learning Forum, 8*(1). Retrieved from www.ntlf.com/html/pi/9812/pbl_1.htm

Roth, W. M., & Bowen, G. M. (1995). Knowing and interacting: A study of culture, practices, and resources in a grade 8 open-inquiry science classroom guided by a cognitive apprenticeship metaphor. *Cognition and Instruction, 13*(1), 73–128.

Rowen, D. (2005). The write motivation using the Internet to engage students in writing across the curriculum. Learning connections—Language arts. *Learning and Leading with Technology, 32*(5), 22–23.

Rule, A., & Barrera, M. (2008). *Three authentic curriculum-integration approaches to bird adaptations that incorporate technology and thinking skills.* Informally published manuscript. University of Northern Iowa, Cedar Falls, IA, Metropolitan State University, Minneapolis, MN. Retrieved from www.eric.ed.gov/PDFS/ED501247.pdf

Salend, S. J. (2009). Technology-based classroom assessments: Alternatives to testing. *Teaching Exceptional Children, 41*(6), 48–59.

Satchwell, R., & Loepp, F. L. (2003). Designing and implementing an integrated mathematics, science, and technology curriculum for the middle school. Retrieved on November 9, 2010, from *Journal of Industrial Teacher Education* at http://scholar.lib.vt.edu/ejournals/JITE/v39n3/satchwell.html

Schlemmer, P., & Schlemmer, D. (2008). *Teaching beyond the test: Differentiated project-based learning in a standards-based age.* Minneapolis, MN: Free Spirit.

Scott, C. (1994). Project-based science: Reflections of a middle school teacher. *The Elementary School Journal, 57*(1), 1–22.

Skylar, A. A., Higgins, K., & Boone, R. (2007). Strategies for adapting webquests for students with learning disabilities. *Intervention in School and Clinic, 43*(1), 20–28.

Stange, E. (2011). Playing in the past. A digital review. *American Heritage, 61*(1), 64–65.

Stepien, W., Gallagher, S., & Workman, D. (1992). *Problem-based learning for traditional and interdisciplinary classrooms.* Aurora: Illinois Mathematics and Science Academy, Center for Problem-Based Learning.

Strobel, J., & van Barneveld, A. (2008). When is PBL more effective? A meta-synthesis of meta-analyses comparing PBL to conventional classrooms. *Interdisciplinary Journal of Problem-based Learning, 3*(1), 44–58.

Tassinari, M. (1996). Hands-on projects take students beyond the book. *Social Studies Review, 34*(3), 16–20.

Thomas, J. W. (2000). *A review of research on project-based learning.* Retrieved on October 25, 2010, from www.bobpearlman.org/bestpractices/PBL_research.pdf

Tomlinson, C. A. (1999). *The differentiated classroom: Responding to the needs of all learners.* Alexandria, VA: Association for Supervision and Curriculum Development.

Tomlinson, C. A. (2010). Differentiating instruction in response to academically diverse student populations. In R. Marzano (Ed.), *On excellence in teaching.* Bloomington, IN: Solution Tree Press.

Tomlinson, C. A., Brimijoin, K., & Narvaez, L. (2008). *The differentiated school: Making revolution changes in teaching and learning.* Alexandria, VA: Association for Supervision and Curriculum Development.

Tsay, M., & Brady, M. (2010). A case study of cooperative learning and communication in pedagogy: Does working in teams make a difference? *Journal of the Scholarship of Teaching and Learning, 10*(2). Retrieved from www.eric.ed.gov/PDFS/EJ890724.pdf

Wachanga, S., & Mwangi, J. (2004). Effects of the cooperative class experiment teaching method on secondary school students' chemistry achievement in Kenya Nakuru district. *International Education Journal, 5*(1). Retrieved from http://ehlt.flinders.edu.au/education/iej/articles/v5n1/wachanga/paper.pdf

Walker, A., & Leary, H. (2008). A problem based learning meta-analysis: Differences across problem types, implementation types, disciplines and assessment levels. *Interdisciplinary Journal of Problem-Based Learning, 3*(1), 12–43.

Waller, L. (2011). Is your kid's classroom connection high speed? Six easy ways to engage students with technology in reading! *Teacher's Workshop Newsletter, 4*(1), 1–3.

Wilmarth, S. (2010). Five socio-technology trends that change everything in teaching and learning. In H. H. Jacobs, *Curriculum 21: Essential education for a changing world.* Alexandria, VA: Association for Supervision and Curriculum Development.

Worthy, J. (2000). Conducting research on topics of student interest. *Reading Teacher, 54*(3), 298–299.

Index

.

CORWIN

A SAGE Company

The Corwin logo—a raven striding across an open book—represents the union of courage and learning. Corwin is committed to improving education for all learners by publishing books and other professional development resources for those serving the field of PreK–12 education. By providing practical, hands-on materials, Corwin continues to carry out the promise of its motto: **"Helping Educators Do Their Work Better."**